Sustainable and affordable housing

RED LOCATION
CULTURAL PRECINCT
noeroarchitects

Samanta Bartocci

con saggi di: Jo Noero, Massimo Faiferri, Fabrizio Pusceddu

CONTENTS

1

Individual freedom and collective bond | 10
Massimo Faiferri

Architecture and Activism | 20
Jo Noero

2

An experience of modification | 28
Samanta Bartocci

Houses and cities: the Pelipe housing | 42
Samanta Bartocci

Memory box: *the Museum of Struggle* | 56
Samanta Bartocci

Living space: the library, archive and art gallery | 76
Samanta Bartocci

3

Spaces of representation: different worlds | 96
Samanta Bartocci

Common ground | 106
Fabrizio Pusceddu

RED LOCATION CULTURAL PRECINCT
noeroarchitects

Architectural Credits: Red Location Cultural Percinct
Client: Nelson Mandela Bay Metropolitan Municipality
Location: New Brighton, Port Elizabeth
Museum: Noero Wolff Architects (Jo Noero [Principal] and Heinrich Wolff) in association with John Blair Architect
Art Gallery, Library and Archive: Noero Wolff Architects (Jo Noero [Principle] and Robert McGiven) in association with John Blair Architect
Note: Noero Wolff Architects has been dissolved. The future work for Red Location will be carried out by Noero Architects.
Civil and Structural Engineers - de Villiers and Hulme
Quantity Surveyors – Bahm, Tayob, Kahn and Matunda
Mechanical and Electrical Engineers – Clinkscales [Eastern Cape]
Heritage consultant – Dr Steven Townsend
Contractor – SBT [Eastern Cape]
Status: Ongoing

PELIP housing
Architects - Noero Wolff Architects - Jo Noero[Principal] Heinrich Wolff, Amit patel, Avish Mistry, Tanzeem rezak, Mara Baum
Client: Swedish International Development Agency
Location: New Brighton, Port Elizabeth
Completion Date: 1999 (built)
Gruppo di progettazione
Jo Noero, Heinrich Wolff, Amit Patel, Avish Mistry, Tanzeem Razak, Mara Baum

Exhibition Credits: Transformation of Red Location

Biennale di Venezia 2012
COMMON GROUND/DIFFERENT WORLDS

Noero Architects, Jo Noero Principal with The Keiskamma Trust, Hamburg, Eastern cape, South africa
Collaborators-Aaron Factor, David Long
Sponsors-Mandela Bay Development Agency

Hand drawing
Jo Noero
"Transformation of Red Location", 2012, ink on paper digital post production printed on canvas, 9.4mx3.5m, Nelson Mandela Bay Municipality
The plan illustrates a new cultural centre in a historic shack settlement, in Port Elizabeth, South Africa a part of the city which was devastated by Apartheid spatial planning.

Tapestry
The Keiskamma Women's Project, Hamburg, Eastern Cape, South africa
"Keiskamma After Guernica", 2009, Re-cycled Textiles Hand Stitched, 7.8mx3.5m.
The Tapestry was made by the Keiskamma Women's Project, Eastern Cape of South Africa. It is based on and is the same size as Picasso's Guernica. The theme is different – the Keiskamma Guernica tackles AIDS/HIV and its impact on South African women.

Credits
All the images and drawings of Red Location Cultural Percinct, belong to Noeroarchitects Archives, courtesy of Jo Noero.

Noero Architects was formed in Johannesburg in 1984. In 2000, the practice relocated to Cape Town, and now has offices in Cape Town and Port Elizabeth. The practice has received both local and international awards, including the Lubetkin Prize from the Royal Institute of British Architects in 2006, the Ralph Erskine Prize from the Nordic Association of Architects in 1993, and the Icon Award for Building of the Year from Icon Magazine in London in 2013.

The work of Noero Architects has been exhibited at the Museum of Modern Art in New York in 2012, the Venice Biennale in 2008, 2010, and 2012, the Singapore Biennale in 2008, the Sao Paolo Biennale in 2009, the Chicago Architecture Biennale in 2015, the Museum of Architecture in Munich in 2014, and the National Gallery of Art in Cape Town in 2009.

The work of the practice has been extensively published and is included in the Phaidon Atlas of 20th Century World Architecture. The work is part of the permanent architecture collection of the Chicago Art Institute.

Jo Noero
Principle
Professional Architect
SACAP, SAIA, CIFA

Noero has designed and built over 200 projects, and has combined a professional career with an academic one, lecturing both locally and internationally.

Noero was the Director of the School of Architecture and Planning at the University of Cape Town from 2000 to 2005. He was a tenured professor at that institution from 2000 to 2015, and is an emeritus professor of the same university.

He was also the Pietro Belluschi Visiting Professor of Design at the University of Oregon in Eugene, Oregon in 2004 and the Ruth and Norman Moore Professor of Architecture and Director of Graduate Studies at Washington University, St Louis, USA from 1996 to 2001.

Noero was awarded the Emma Smith Art Scholarship for overseas study from The University of Natal, where he also received the Professor Alexander Petrie Award for Outstanding Contribution to the Arts and Humanities in 1997.

In 1994, Noero received an Honorary Doctorate of Science from Brighton University. He was elected as an Honorary Fellow of the Royal Institute of British Architects in 2001 and an International Fellow in 2010. He was also elected as an Honorary Fellow of the American Institute of Architects in 2015. Noero was elected a Fellow of the Academy of Science of South Africa in 2001, received the Gold Medal for Architecture from the South African Institute of Architects in 2010, and is an Alumnus of the Salzburg Seminar.

Red Location Cultural Precinct and the informal dwelling

Red Location Cultural Precinct

Individual freedom and collective bond

Underlying urban planning there is the same objective as in a democracy worthy of its name: to establish a balance between individual freedom and collective bond. It is a difficult problem that will never be able to be solved once and for all.
Everything depends however on the limits within which it can be achieved. In other words: the condition of a civilisation depends on the degree to which a chaotic mass can be transformed into an integrated, vital community. In any case, the prerequisite for this is that human attitude be recognised first of all as having the right of primogeniture, of leadership.
Siegfried Giedion[1]

With these words one of the most authoritative scholars and theorists of the Nineteen hundreds analyses, with the passion of the observer immersed in his own times, the new aspects introduced into architecture and urban planning by technological development. His proposal for a new regionalism, a modern, authentic, monumental spirit, and the need for a new collective conscience lead with almost utopian dynamism the ideal image of the city of the future. A humanised city, both in its living spaces and community outreach places, one able to satisfy those aesthetic values that are the true needs of an individual and a collectivity. A city that cannot be conceived as a simple economic, geographical or climatic phenomenon, but must above all be thought of as a social phenomenon. An urban planner siding with this humanisation process needs firstly to try to solve the problem, enquiring into what the structure of today's city should be, in order to restore the balance between individual freedom and collective bond.
A recent reflection by Rahul Mehrotra[2] appears to be able to help us analyse the features of this dilemma better, highlighting the numerous forms of urbanisation that share the same physical space in most contemporary cities. These heterogeneous paradigms of city development alternate between the physical figure of the formal or static city and the temporal horizon of the informal or kinetic city. It is indeed in these urban landscapes present on all continents that the kinetic or informal city is becoming a symbolic image and metaphor of the physical condition characterising

1. Siegfried Giedion, Architektur und Gemeinschaft, 1956, Italian translation: *Breviario di architettura*, Bollati Boringhieri, Turin, 2008
2. Rahul Mehrotra, Re-thinking the informal city, in *AREA*, 2013, 128, pp.6-11.

Massimo Faiferri

the contemporary city. Perhaps it is an excessive simplification of the flexible complexity of contemporary urban landscapes, but it proves very useful for tackling the theme of urban transformation and its relationship with the social reality of a context. The static city clearly consists of its architecture and its most permanent materials like concrete, steel and bricks and has always represented the preferred key to interpreting urban environments. At the same time, a new fluctuating reality is emerging in our cities, a three-dimensional construct developing progressively, built of lighter, sometimes recycled, materials, which changes and reinvents itself constantly. *"But however much the static city owes its representation to architecture, this is no longer the only key to reading urban reality. The kinetic city however, is not perceived in architectural terms but rather in terms of spaces that have their own associative value and support daily existence. Models for occupation determine their shape and the perception of them. In this case it is a question of indigenous urbanisation that has its own particular local logic."* This process highlights the issue of simultaneousness and coexistence, opening the way to new challenges in planning or replanning cities, in which it will be more and more necessary to give a formal character to the spatial configuration by which this simultaneousness is achieved, reconsidering the urban condition in terms of economy, legality, activism, governance and collaboration.
It is thus a renewed challenge for the project, which will need to conceive of places and forms that could take on social significance, trying to satisfy in the best way possible the needs of the people who will be using those spaces. A project that will necessarily need to go beyond the autonomous architectural form that transcends its time and place, trying instead to establish what is fixed and inviolable and what can, on the other hand, be adapted to different uses over time, with continuous alternation between the features of the static city (and its architecture) and the kinetic city with its particular fluctuating local reality. *"It is a challenge at the centre of which lies a not insignificant question: the capacity of architecture to offer protection and be useful, but to also have the possibility to change and adapt itself over time."* Some architects have agreed to openly handle these themes, relaunching with their projects a further contribution linked with the specificity of the contexts in which they are working. Planners who act on an urban stage where difficult local situations coexist, characterised

Overall view of Red Location Cultural Precinct and its spatial impact

by complex social issues with a turbulent past and the ubiquitous effects of globalisation.

Thanks to the many initiatives organised at the ecourbanlab[3], the Department of Architecture Design and Urban Planning's research lab in Alghero, during the past few years I have had the fortune and privilege to be able to study Jo Noero's work in depth, to listen to his lectures and analyse his drawings and pictures displayed at the exhibitions accompanying his classes at the Master in Sustainable and Affordable Housing. From the moment I met him I was fascinated by his personality: a very inquisitive man, with an uncommon creative streak and speed of reflection, and a great willingness to discuss his ideas. As I observed his work and listened to his explanations, his fascinating research emerged on the necessary, unambiguous bond architecture involves. A vision of the architect building each time for a definite place and role, in an inextricable relationship between his own being and doing, who wants to have his position in society clear. An architect who enquires not only into the instruments but also the contexts of his work and the origins of collective formal and symbolic features.

In his projects Noero uses readable, understandable forms, onto which shared symbols and meanings can be projected. It is narrative architecture called up to construct social symbols, which develops a story at the different scales of the project. An architect/builder who creates spaces and not drawings of facades. Spaces that fill themselves with meanings brought by the people who use them.

At our various meetings over these past years a dialogue developed between us in which architecture was linked with a reflection on our own being, our own experience and the places and people that surround us and remind us of the profoundly human and collective values of design.

At the same time, I was able to appreciate his passion and talent for teaching. In his lectures and the planning workshops he led, his desire strongly emerged to involve students in a process that could go beyond the fascination of form, to focus on other spheres of practice not dominated exclusively by planning problems. His stories about practising the profession in South Africa opened up a reflection on the role of the university and education of the architect. Many questions and thoughts were brought up. Among them I remember bewilderment over the educational syllabuses proposed by the schools of architecture, which basically addressed a nostalgic past and were lacking in the contents necessary for an open encounter with our contemporary times. His criticism seemed significant to me of the idea of individual genius, still widespread at many universities but now surpassed in a globally-connected world, in which new complex

3. www.ecourbanlab.it

problems are emerging that cannot be tackled except through the ties of cooperative and collaborative work. The sort of work necessary to produce a kind of architecture appreciated by the public and able to show society the value of this profession.

A profession that, for Noero, needs to enquire into the profoundly human and collective worth of *doing* at all scales of design. All his projects respond to this deep feeling, for his architecture has strong urban belonging, conceived and designed to accommodate man and his purposes. Noero's architecture is made to welcome life, and the buildings and spaces his projects contain take on meaning from the activities developing inside them. Life is also convention, habit, way of being and doing, both of the individual and of a community. For life to unfold inside them, buildings need to spread their spaces out in a logical system of sequences, of separate and sharing elements arranged in various ways throughout. For Noero architecture is not just construction of forms. Architecture can contribute to economic and cultural development and can affect the life of the local population.

The Red Location project published in this book was devised for one of the key places of South African history, the symbol of the struggle against apartheid. This district was the focal point of a vast plan to recuperate and celebrate memory. Noero's project tells us of the collective struggles of this people, the invisible structures of power that defined the social experience of apartheid and the promise of a cultural identity. Despite the fact that to a distracted observer the buildings constructed might bring figurative imagery to mind, the project had the capacity to refer to the features of local buildings and to pre-existing spatial relations, linking up with the local social and economic reality. It is design centred on the community: an authentic civic project where the planner has had to learn to see, and to listen, so as to subsequently be able to present a proposal able to express the difficulties and frustrations, but also the joys and values, of those inhabiting these places. In its shape the museum building recalls the industrial architectures beside which the South African townships arose, and it stages without rhetoric the contradictions of the past and current conditions of poverty. It is a project deriving not just from a rigorous description of the culture and society studied by the architect, but from a "negotiation of meanings" that takes place in the changing contingencies of work in the field; negotiation between the architect's personality, cultural baggage and roles he undertakes, and the different ones of the interlocutors he enters into dialogue with.

The project's worth is also highly symbolic; its prerequisite for improving the conditions of the township is the growth of a sense of belonging and the creation of a collective conscience of the inhabitants, with the setting up of representative public elements. In carrying out a task that is quite obvious, but not to be taken for granted, the project tries to present itself as a tool to improve the social, political and economic conditions of a place by involving the interested parties in a constructive project process, and through awareness-raising among community members in an emancipatory cultural process. As Noero himself says: *"at the heart of everything that we do as architects is the desire to make architecture that is culturally and socially satisfying"*.

Ethical causes in architecture, and not only architecture, are a delicate matter since they clash with the still unsolved question of the relations and interference between morality and art, between ethics and aesthetics. In a cultural context like our contemporary one ethics seems prevalently an alternative to aesthetics, where all the models and interpretative instruments devised not in vain to bring us close to beauty have not been able to contribute to an exhaustive definition of it. Jo Noero's projects however, manage to bring the concept of beautiful in architecture close to an ethics of planning, aimed at satisfying clear needs and necessities. In his works architecture undoubtedly possesses a civic value, since it is considered a patrimony of the city and its community. Perhaps it will indeed be up to the ethics of good construction to discriminate between good and bad architecture in the conviction that – to paraphrase Plato – if "Beauty is the splendour of truth", we should all retrieve beauty in its intrinsic meaning, as harmony of man with himself and with the environment surrounding him, as an elevated form of civilisation.

From this point of view, the numerous initiatives that the ecourbanlab research lab has organised in recent years with Jo Noero, from which this book originates, have also put the extreme need to inhabit at the centre of attention. It has urged planning research to focus again on this theme in disciplinary reasoning. There are therefore historic reasons why in the last decades of the Nineteen hundreds the theme of inhabiting as a necessity was in a certain sense elusive. It was so because the concept of necessity itself was elusive, perhaps because, as we have already said, its spatial reference, the city, had become increasingly different to understand. The classical practices in planning living space seem to have difficulty in accounting for such a volatile, abstract urban model. Numerous proposals have tried to draw close to the phenomenon with a variety of instruments, but in no case were they devised to satisfy traditional necessities. The need to find once more a focus for disciplinary research in *necessity*, a compass able to steer us in our action, is suggested to us by numerous exhibitions, publications and urban transformation interventions that seek to expand the inhabiting concept, evoking a correlation with Heidegger's meaning of inhabiting as taking care of reality, inhabiting as new attention to reality, its inherent necessariness, as part of the non-negotiable values of our urban perspectives. Noero's projects investigate this deep meaning and urge us as scholars to tackle this moral imperative, this emergency of inhabiting[4]. The widespread insistence on entrusting the prospects of evolution and solution of these aspects to the objects of architecture has deeply modified forms and modalities of the project, generating a clear detachment from the ethics and social legitimisation of planners. From this point of view, this publication should be given credit for having contributed to nurturing the disciplinary reflection on these works and the themes springing from them. The projects presented in this book try to fill the distance from this renunciation of individual and collective responsibility, and from the loss of the general sense of one's action and its effects. This detachment has quite deep relations with inhabiting and its emergencies; it calls for the project to make a moral commitment to transform the environment in which we live. As Noero says: *"The lesson of Red Location is that South Africa is a country with a tumultuous history marked by the striving of various groups to be free. However, freedom should never come at the expense of any other group of people. To be free is to be able to offer to others the possibility to be free."* The theory not written, but built in this place by Jo Noero, may, I think, well represent this noble intention.

---

[4]. See on this matter: Jo Noero, Housing in the post modern world, in Massimo Faiferri, Samanta Bartocci, *Housing the Emergency - The Emergency of Housing*, ListLab, Trento, 2012 p.148

"Transformation of Red Location", Biennale di Venezia, Common ground/different worlds, L 9.4×3.5m, hand drawing , ink on paper, digital post production, printed on Textile

©naero architects archives

Architecture and Activism

It seems to me to be reasonable that we consider architecture as an art that is brought into being in order to satisfy some kind of ethical good – if not I would argue it cannot meet the needs of architecture.
Early architectural theorists wrote that architecture was a practical art brought into being for a purpose other than for its own satisfaction – this condition one could argue does not apply to any one of the fine arts other than architecture.
Contemporary architecture has become commodified and preoccupied with representing itself as iconic: this concerns me. More worrying is the idea that architects and critics refer to community architecture as if it was something apart from architecture itself. My practice was recently invited to submit work for a global award for so called community architecture – we told the organizers we were not interested. We don't see ourselves as community architects or activist architects or whatever – we are architects making architecture which is beautiful and socially purposeful, (and seeks) to meet the needs of the people using the spaces.
There are many misconceptions about architecture that have arisen over the last fifty years or so and have led to this predicament. These issues lead us away from an understanding one could argue is a necessary pre-condition for authentic architectural work.

First misconception

We need to differentiate our roles as citizens and as architects. I don't believe that one can affect political change through architecture – however it is clear to me that one can, through the exercise of one's citizenship, contribute to effective societal change. Difficulties emerge for architects when their political convictions collide with their work. It is at this point that one is called upon to make an ethical judgment about the kind of work one is prepared to do as an architect. In this regard there can be no rules - one necessarily makes up ones own rules according to his or her value system. For example, in my practice we have the rule that we will not design a house larger than 150 squared meters – the reason for this is that in a world of diminishing resources, we don't believe that anyone should have the right to live in a house bigger than this size. Similarly, we will not work for people who see our labour only in terms of profit maximization.

Jo Noero
Noero Architects[1]

Second misconception
Peter Eisenman and others have made a pernicious contribution to the idea that architectural form is autonomous and carries within it only geometry as a regulating idea to give shape to form. This cannot be since without purpose architecture cannot exist. It seems to me that the more difficult question is evaded by these hollow arguments. The quest should be to establish both what is fixed and inviolable and what can adjust to different uses over time. This is a challenge and at the heart of this challenge is the difficult question about the architecture's ability to shelter, be useful, and also to offer the possibility of change and adaptation over time. Surely at the heart of everything that we do as architects is the desire to make our work culturally and socially satisfying, and most importantly able to adjust to change over time.

Third misconception
For who is the work of architecture intended? The focus on autonomous forms has reduced architecture to hollow sculpture – we no longer talk to the people using our buildings since this makes the process of design messy and complicated. When we build office buildings or factories, architects generally don't speak to the unions representing the workers – I suspect that that does not happen very often – yet these are the people who occupy the spaces that we make. I saw a recent documentary about a house designed by OMA in which the domestic worker was interviewed – her life was a miserable one because the architecture had not taken into account the domestic difficulties associated with cleaning the house. I can imagine the architect's response – with an arrogant sneer he / she would probably exclaim that the needs of art are not served by the messiness of everyday living – too bad since that kind of view relegates architecture to sculpture and not much else.

Fourth misconception
Architectural form is autonomous and transcends its time and place. This argument was well illustrated by Ionesco in a famous passage where he wrote about a beautiful church that had become a place of incarceration

1. The text that follows is a reworking of themes dealt with by the same author in *Lotus 145*, 2011.

and torture during a revolutionary moment in time – he raised the issue about the ability of good architecture to both transcend use and time. What Ionesco did not deal with is the ethical dimension of architecture, which is a trans-active one, and which lies in the relationship between the commissioner of the work and the architect. It is precisely at this moment that the architect is called upon to make an ethical judgment about whether to proceed with the commission. That judgment must be shaped by the nature of the commission and its purpose. It is of no ethical consequence what uses the spaces assumes after this moment since it is beyond the control of the architect and the client. This point is crucial: I lived in South Africa through the Apartheid era and many well intentioned architects accepted work from the Apartheid government with the mistaken belief that it would be given a useful purpose following the country's liberation. This might have been true in some cases but it still represents an ethical quandary, since those architects acted unprofessionally and unethically in accepting these commissions. OMA's rationale for designing the Chinese Broadcasting Center in Beijing is not so different from the arguments put forward by those architects who collaborated with the apartheid regime or those who worked with the Nazis during World War 2.

Fifth misconception
Architectural form is ethical – this is not so – architectural form is built, material fact – architectural form is inanimate and only assumes value through human agency. It can symbolize at a moment in time a particular set of social and power relations but these relationships can dissolve in a moment. The only certain ethical relationship that can exist in architecture is a contractual one binding architect and client together – this ethical relationship is also very clearly linked to the nature of the program offered by the client. In my practice we have faced this issue many times and have refused commissions because we didn't believe that the project's purposes would have been socially productive or in the best interests of the wider community. It is in this realm that activism and architecture come together.

Sixth misconception
Ethics and architecture don't mix – this is the refrain that architects employ all the time – it is good to talk about activism and architecture but architects need to make a living and if this means to sit down with the devil then so be it. It seems to me that there is no question of choice in this matter – one simply cannot accept unethical commissions: it is a matter of conscience and there cannot be compromise.

Seventh misconception

This deals with pushing the present into the future, employed very successfully by many so-called global star-architects. The line of reasoning goes as follows - I know that the building's purpose is immoral but the ownership/use will change and lead to more   benevolent uses over time. This is based on the idea that the future will be better than the present. Given the experience of the twentieth century, we know this to be untrue in most cases. The future is uncertain and many projects undertaken in the twentieth century - both spatial and political - with an optimistic set of future goals turned out to be catastrophic. The only ethical way of acting in the world is to accept present time and everyday existence, and to always consider that in one's work. Everything except the present is uncertain – it could be argued that even the present is unknowable but at least it exists in real time.

Eighth misconception

Ethically based architecture is ugly. It seems as if the architectural world divides those architects who make great form from those who are socially committed to working through architecture to make better spaces for people. The fact that the two can co-exist and that the aim of all good architecture should be to ensure that this happens does not figure in the minds of critics and architects alike. For example, recently we participated in the Small Scale, Big Change exhibition at MOMA in New York. The curator, Andres Lepik, intended to demonstrate that architecture can make change for the better and that architecture itself could be beautiful and pleasing. In the New York Times, the architectural critic prefaced his review with the condescending statement that some of the work in the show was surprisingly good. This patronizing statement represented everything that is wrong for me with the prevailing value system in architecture, namely that good works in the ethical sense are generally considered not to be fine works of architecture - when one finds examples of beautiful socially responsive architecture, the work is held as the exception rather than the rule. This is sad.

Conclusion

Architecture has been reified and relegated to the status of a commodity produced for its novelty value and not much else. It has been argued that so-called autonomous architecture devoid of any purpose other than its own rules of geometry - whether these rules are Cartesian or Algorithmic - cannot be held to be architecture. Architecture involves engagement with the world of people and their needs, likes and dislikes. Failure to engage with these issues will not only produce architecture devoid of meaning but it will also be unethical.

The "original" rusty iron house in Red Location

2

An experience of modification

Photographer David Goldblatt was attracted by ´stillness and banality´. Between 1964 and 1993 he traced the history of South Africa intercepting in the *architecture of the diverse and complex communities* of that country the following question: "*How is it possible to be law abiding, normal, and descent in a society and in a system that is fundamentally evil?*"[1]. The subjects, houses, public residences, governmental buildings, re-establishment communities, Dutch Reformed churches and monuments, are the enduring expression of South Africa's ethics and morality, as well as the revelation of how ideology has shaped the landscape in many ways. The pictures enclose "*the structure of things*", as defined by Goldblatt himself, social and super-structures as *manifest symbol* of the conditions that have created them. These images explore how the people's[2] values, their ethics, their aspirations, fears and needs have taken shape in the constructed areas of South Africa.

At the end of the last millennium, when South Africa was reinventing itself as multicultural, anti-racist and democratic, another artist captured the "*spirit of time*": J. Alexander focuses on the daily conditions and deep political changes that the country was experiencing. *The Butcher Boys* (1985-86) and the *Bom Boys*[3] (1998) are among the most representative expressions of the evils of apartheid: full-scale sculptures of children, the ´humans-in-the-making', who challenge categorisation, neo-colonialist domination; the growing obsession for security and the simultaneous global proliferation of borders and surveillance systems.

Goldblatt's pictures and Alexander's sculptures fully evoke South Africa's

---

1. *Apartheid, White Society and Photography*, interview to David Goldblatt at the 2016 Arles Festival, France. The interview was conducted by Laetitia Martinez and recorded in Arles by Cedric Batifoulier, on the occasion of the 2006 Retrospective of David Goldblatt, directed by Martin Paar.
2. The reference to David Goldblatt's work (currently exhibiting at the Centre Pompidou in Paris) introduces the South African context, in paarticular Red Location Cultural Precinct. We also remember David Goldblatt's photographs depicting the stories of some activists who thought for the country's transition, at the Exhibitions on Port Elizabeth in the Red Location Museum: *David Goldblatt, "1990 Activists – Port Elizabeth; Uitenhage"* (2008). The pictures were originally for the Human Rights Watch magazine "Monitor", but were never published.
3. Bom Boys (1998) is a full-scale sculpture of children, placed on a big chessboard wearing animal masks; it is inspired to a gang of street children who defended a street in the centre of Cape City where Jane Alexander lived. In this sense, its 'human values' symbolise and induce us to reflect on the permeable borders separating the human from the animal world.

Samanta Bartocci

apartheid, a context in which Jo Noero worked since the 80's, moving between the duplicity of the two communities' spaces (black and white). He always traced in the project and the architecture, theory and practice in the architect's profession, a continuous cycle of knowledge production, endlessly permeated by an 'independent critical conscience'. (Ward, 1969) Of course, the purpose is to respond to emergencies, but also to walk down roads and reach authentic gratitude, giving birth to practices and active forms of planning from an urban space and architectural perspective.

The contemporary South African context is certainly complex: *a land of opportunities and in exponential growth in the next years, especially referring to a slowly emerging middle class of the new conurbations, with its growing desires and material needs*[4] *[...]*
A slow though relentless political stabilization in the majority of central and south African countries is stimulating social growth in these areas and the possibility of conceiving them not in terms of emergency but of normality, in spite of currently dramatic and chronicle levels of corruption and socioeconomic imbalances. (Molinari, 2013)
Inconceivable for some people, the end of apartheid has allowed the development of South Africa. Transition from an authoritarian regime to a democracy has harboured the paradigm of equality between victims and executioners, and the hierarchy of differences has found a fertile space and context to grow in.
Urban issues clearly show the sign of the post-colonial years but the post-apartheid buildings are still a relevant one at present.
Architecture and urban spaces clearly respond to the strategies of urban exclusion, social hierarchy, segregation and marginalisation fostered by the laws and the apartheid government. Power expressed in all its strategic representations, at all scales. Body and soul, city and land.
In this context, the segmentation of the boundaries from the *other* has rep-

---

4. *However, Africa is also the continent of a new, aggressive form of territorial and economic neo-colonialism: several major powers such as China, Saudi Arabia, Qatar, South Korea and the United States, are purchasing thousands of acres of virgin land through their multinational corporations, imagining a near future where water and food will progressively be lacking. Tornare all'Africa e alla sua architettura*, L. Molinari (2013) - https://www.ilpost.it/lucamolinari/2013/12/27/tornare-allafrica-alla-architettura/

Red Location Cultural Precinct and New Brighton

resented the place of limitation and suspension; in these terms, the exercise of segregation circumscribed the *space of the city for the black people* from the *real space of the white* South Africans. However, the need for distinction and to exercise the strategy of spatial exclusion did not found itself on the concept of distance but on a form of controlled proximity. (Secchi, 2013)

The 'double-landscape' syndrome has been well described by Lisa Findley in *Building Change: Architecture, Politics and Cultural Agency*. It was developed in 1948, when the nationalists took power and introduced apartheid. *"Apartheid" is an Afrikaner word meaning "separation", and a large proportion of its laws and policies were about formalizing the already existent and longstanding practices of racial segregation in South Africa. The consequences were devastating for a vast majority of the nation's people and for its future. Apartheid was a kind of super-segregation that also served as a strategy for economic and spatial exploitation. After the 1948 election, the Parliament rapidly passed a series of Acts that further spatialized segregation— at all scales from the body to the nation— and resulted in the transfer of huge tracts of lands out of black and colored ownership and control."* (Findley, 2005 p. 131)

Under colonial rule, South Africa was a country already heavily divided, with an unequal society. In 1927, in fact, the government had forbidden sexual intercourse between black and white people. The rationalisation of separation was intensified after the nationalist party's election in 1948. A series of prohibiting acts became racist laws, starting from the *Mixed Marriage Act* (1949), an extensive ban to marriages eventually resulting in the formalisation of the *Population Registration Act* (1950), considered the true strength of apartheid. All individuals had to be registered and classified as 'white', 'black' or 'coloured', and later on as 'Asian' or 'Indian'. Following the *Group Areas Act* (1950), other laws brought to forced dislocation of communities, in specifically designed areas, among which the desirable urban and suburban ones were destined only to the 'white'.

"This resulted in new dislocations of entire communities. It also broke up thriving multi-ethnic communities. Long Standing neighborhoods, with the bad fortune to be on lands wanted by the white elite, were bulldozed. The new black and colored segregated communities, moved to more marginal land some distance from the white areas, were then given separate schools and other public facilities of sub-standard quality compared to what white communities had". (Findley, 2005 p.132)

The evident dark side of power of the apartheid era[5] (1948-1994) planned and built the urban residential model called *'township'*, which included, be-

---

5. Apartheid *legally* ended in 1994 and with the new constitution entering into force millions of black people voted for the first time in their lives. On 10th May of the same year Nelson Mandela became President of South Africa.

sides homes, dormitories, schools, services and all diverse activities. Access to public libraries or museums was forbidden; the rules on permits were very clear about the confinement to the area of identification and residence. The urban segregation has left its traces also in the idea of public space. A kind of *"amnesia[6] of the meaning"* of what is public space appears as a suspended memory in the fracture imposed by apartheid.

The strong spatial moulds preserve, especially in the *townships*, their roots in the contemporary urban areas, resistant to continuous modifications and predominantly poor. It is important to remember that the *'township or ex township's'* peripheral dimension is not made of spaces antithetic to the *'city of the white'* (today, simply of the rich) but maintains the features of an urban, simultaneously present, though reciprocally impenetrable, exclusive reality. In this way, the debate on the post-apartheid urbanity moves from the image of a successful ideology of segregation to the current strategy of spatial segmentation, which is increasing for disparity of wealth, strengthened by the city's infrastructural weaknesses and inaccessibility, and rather eased by the request for new houses in the townships.

The territory of these cities can be represented as the combination of *"fragments connected to each other only by infrastructural networks, productive and residential areas separated by protective and exclusive borders"* (Magnaghi, 2003). It is dismantled into a plurality of complex urban identities that foster dynamism and highlight a certain degree of instability. The city lives an informal evolution with and around the colonial city.

What is left of the spatial consequentiality's structure in the (usual) post-colonial African city is the picture of people in expansion and in movement. *"The never-ending appropriation and recovery of space defines the urban schemes and keeps the city in a constant state of renovation."* (Moronell, 2011)

Where the city marks its multiple transcultural identities in space, towards a 're-planning´ of it, the public (or collective) space represents an essential element for the creation of ways to live together, in its inclusive and potential meaning.

In this context, concepts such as Culture, History and Public Area, elsewhere contested or simply revisited, are central of daily life in post-apartheid South Africa; elements able to understand the city's meaning in its entirety. If on the one side, we could affirm that a contemporary city organizes its spatial models in a dispersive, mobile and 'individualising' manner, denying the role of the public, and of its space in a collective dimension; on

---

6. For a better insight on the meaning of amnesia and memory in the scope of architecture, see *Recycled Theory: Dizionario illustrato/Illustrated* Dictionary, S. Marini, G. Corbellini, Quodlibet, Macerata, 2016, p. 35.

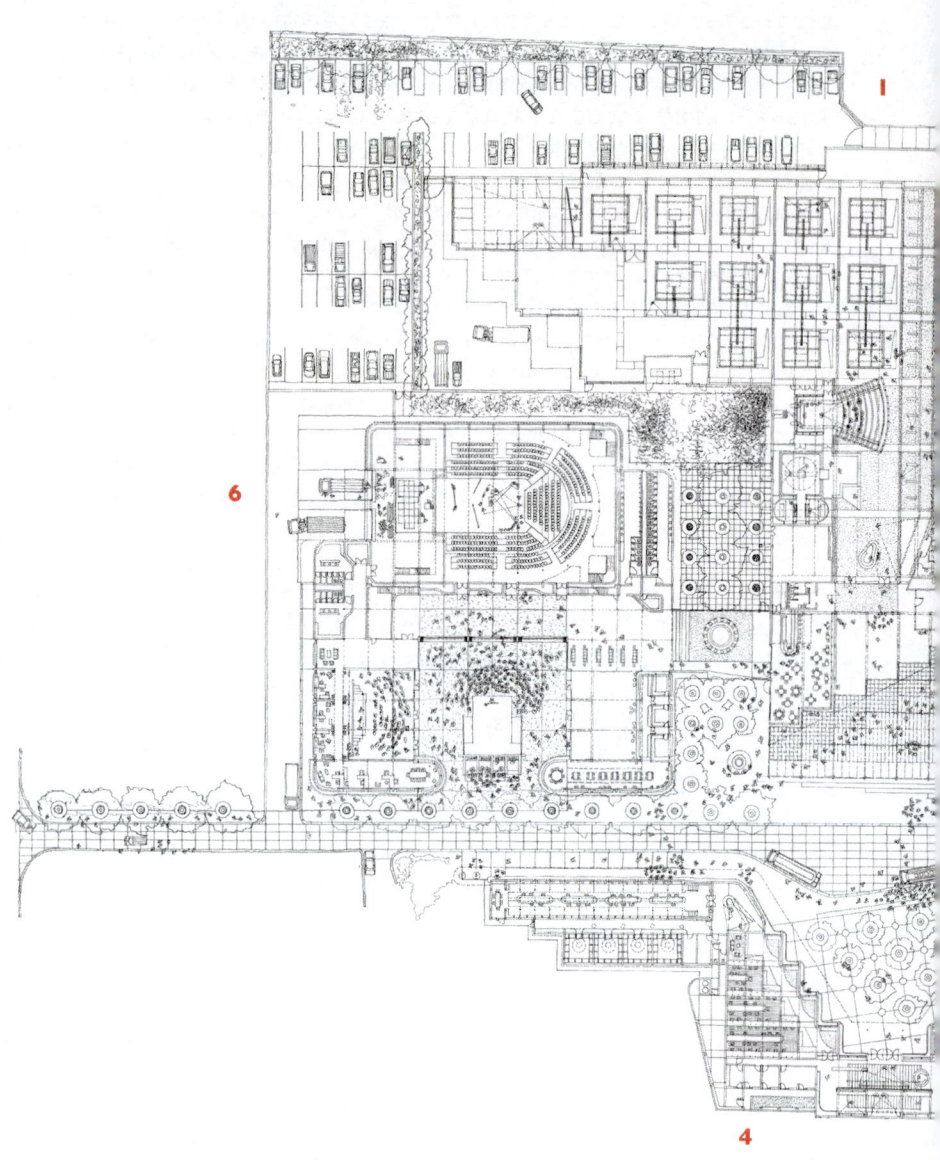

34   Red Location Cultural Precinct

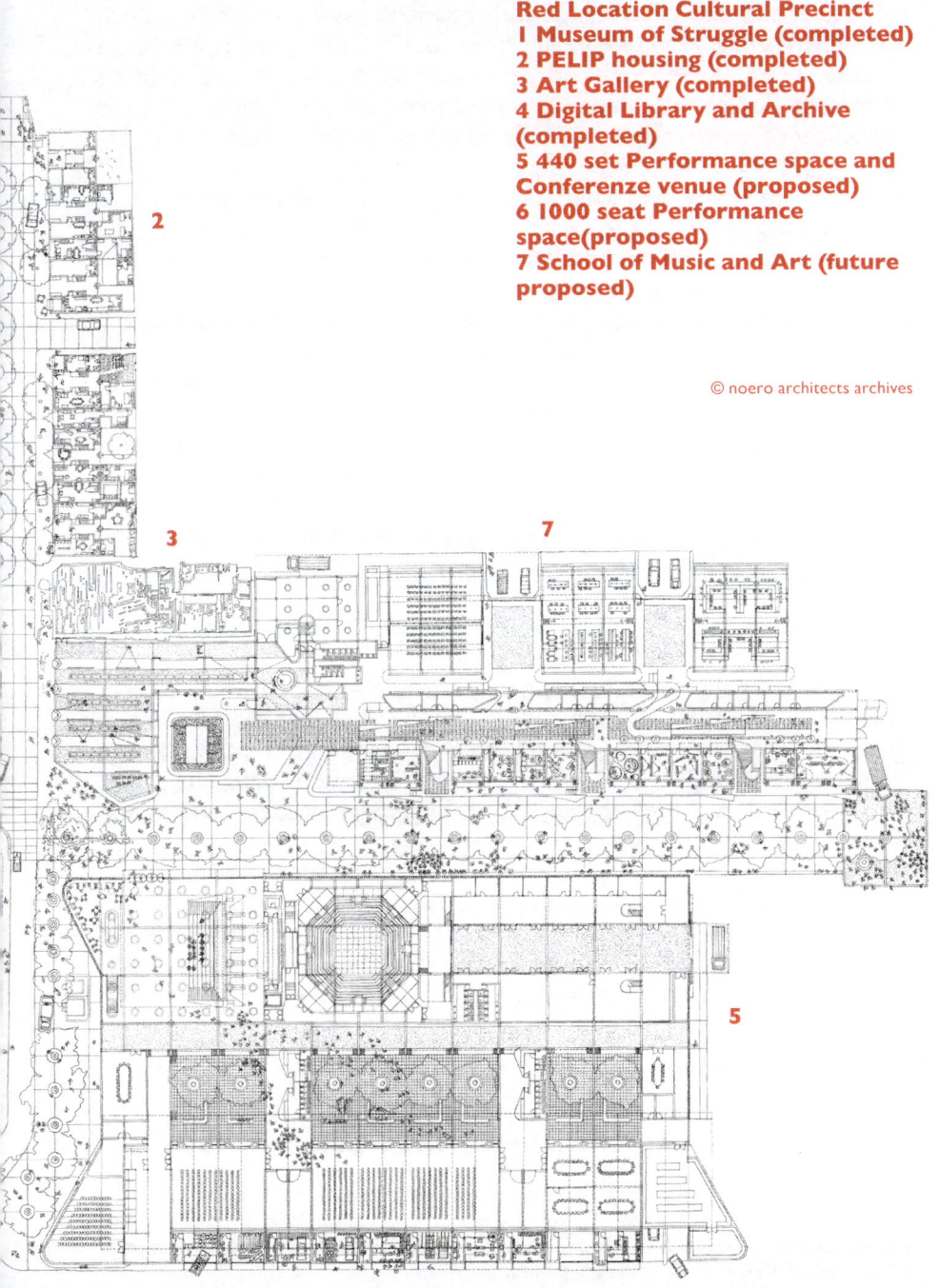

Red Location Cultural Precinct
1 Museum of Struggle (completed)
2 PELIP housing (completed)
3 Art Gallery (completed)
4 Digital Library and Archive (completed)
5 440 set Performance space and Conferenze venue (proposed)
6 1000 seat Performance space (proposed)
7 School of Music and Art (future proposed)

© noero architects archives

the other, a community on the move appropriates spaces, it models them to make them habitable and eventually open to public use. Since South Africa renewed into a multicultural and democratic society, we started to find a permanent workshop of ways of living together; we can observe individual and collective experiences embracing otherness, empathy, dignity and freedom in light of those dramatic events.

Starting from the visceral role that culture, memory, history and public space have in daily life, these concepts are re-interpreted in the project for Red Location's cultural area, assuming that architecture clearly produces a crucial effect on our transformation.

Introducing this extraordinary project, we wish to remind that the majority of South African histories of struggle began right in the heart of Red Location in New Brighton, where the first forms of passive, non violent resistance and civil disobedience organized by the African National Congress (ANC)[7] took place. The first act of the 'Defiance Campaign' in 1952 saw Raymond Mhlaba cross the station's "Whites Only" entrance (previously home to the first MK unit). The resistance was organized in small 'cells' protected by the basements dug under the houses in Red Location. Within these cells, leaders such as Nelson Mandela, Walter Sisulu and Govan Mbecki were present.

Apartheid ended 40 years later and Port Elizabeth had its first non-racist local government ('Transitional Representative Council'), ready to face the issue of New Brighton's disadvantaged context, in a kind of revitalizing plan to recreate a balance with the City of Port Elizabeth. At the same time, the government and municipality chose Red Location to be the space of memorial. With this decision in mind, many sites were built, assuming that the investment in spaces of remembrance, such as museums and theme parks, would have brought a return in economic and touristic terms. This did not occur in the short term.

In 1998, Noero Wolff Architects' studio won the contest for the *Red Location Cultural Precinct* project. The studio gave birth to an extraordinary

---

7. The party was founded in 1912 to defend the rights and freedoms of the black majority. Right after 1948, the ANC began its non-violent protest against the government's decisions and laws, reaching international exposure. When the repression intensified and began violent (one of the first massacres took place in Soweto in 1976 in defence of the black population's education standards) many anti-apartheid political leaders were banned, exiled or hidden. Nelson Mandela and the other activists were sentenced to life imprisonment in 1963. From that moment and until 1980, South Africa experienced a time of brutality, conflicts, strikes, rallies and insurrections at all levels. State of emergency was declared in 1985, until the election of the new president F.W. de Klerk in 1989. His first reformist decisions were Nelson Mandela's release, the legalization of the ANC party and the revocation of the apartheid laws. In 1991, the works for a new constitution and for a transitional plan to a new South Africa began.

public structure composed by the Apartheid Museum (known as the Museum of struggle), an art-gallery, a library and new houses, all with a low budget and great civil respect. Noero Wolff Architects' planning process became embedded in Red Location's context, never losing sight of it, and tenaciously identifying the city's strength in the civic dimension (although several projects are still waiting to be realised).

The point of view of the projects is based on the observation of the different forms of *spatialization* of the contemporary urban condition, aware of the fact that territories cannot choose the circumstances but can confront their heritage. Jo Noero states that *"architecture should be a means to open minds."* Under this point of view, the project's effort is turned towards offering old and new inhabitants the possibility to familiarise with open-mindedness and the freedom offered by public spaces in the territory. These sites are free to visit and offer to men a land of opportunity where they can play an active role in *"creating an urban path."* (Choay, 1994)

By dealing with all South Africa's contradictions, and the strategies for international commemorations and presentations, *"Noero wonders, 'what is the fitting memorial that will trigger the past for the largely poor, uneducated populace that has never stepped inside a museum before?' This question was the generative concept that Noero and his firm embraced as they joined other cultural institutions in South Africa subscribing to a post-apartheid national heritage agenda'."* (Heath, 2009 p.76)

In 1998, the progress-driven policies were coupled to the reality perceived by the architectures, which showed how 65% of the South African population was living in informal 'hand-made' *bidonvilles*[8]. 90% of the population had been prevented to access public buildings and museums until 1994, so did know nothing about them. In this critical context, Noero Wolffs Architects' project proceeds[9] bearing in mind the principles inspiring all the different construction phases in Red Location.

The first issue concerns the plurality of urban scales, observable in the variety of spaces requested by the tender; in the complexity and vast dimensions of the museum area; and in the uncultivated land in between houses as the only public space.

8. Recent census state that 11% of the South African urban population lives in *informal housing*; the levels of inequality and redistribution of richness are among the highest in the world.
9. Red Location spreads on an area of only 1.45 squared kilometres in the township of New Brighton, and has a population of 15.286 inhabitants. New Brighton's current extension is 4.2 km, 20 times bigger than the original area. Red Location's toponym is still very known among the local population; moreover, since the construction of Red Location Cultural Precinct (1999), Red Location's area has progressively acquired a broader importance and its toponym identified an area bigger than the original one (Montanini, 2016).

In this context, we can exclude the search for a formal public space or the memorial's emblem. On the contrary, we can understand how a public space can concentrate the passiveness of meanings and offer to figures in the public that inclusive, connective and organising power able to overturn the paradigm that sees the market laws guiding the morphologies and lifestyles in contemporary cities.

The public dimension and the system to build "ways to live together" may develop in this context. Space has this features, as stated by Lefebvre; after all, New Brighton is a place in which oral traditions and memories of the apartheid are still vivid. When the inhabitants were asked which heritage better represented the opposition to apartheid, the majority of them replied that New Brighton was one of the first entirely black South African cities. When the Group Areas Act, in charge of dividing the people by race, applied the redistribution in New Brighton, the non-black residents were obliged to leave, leaving behind the remains of an intact community that grew in the context of resistance and then in the disobedience of 1952.

By asking himself "*how do we represent the 'public' in architecture?*", Jo Noero finds three 'archetypes' in the Council of the South African Union's Union's posters (1980); houses with one floor; schools with two floors; the factory's roof. With these images widespread in the inhabitants' memory, the project not only has to represent the economical and political analysis of space but sets also the target of modelling the historical shape in the economical and political territory of the State that has repeatedly reproduced it.

In *Red Location Cultural Precinct*, the spatial representation follows the place-making politics in a suitable and recognizable design, as to make '*people understand right away*'[10], to mention Lefebvre again. An everyday ethics leading to a kind of celebration of ordinary materials, the same used to build factories and houses, the workplace and civic virtues.

---

10. Place-making describes a methodological approach to the redefinition of public spaces, where the design is linked to the user's needs, and space is conceived as flexible, welcoming, but especially attractive and able to create growth in those urban areas. This concept was first described in the works of Jane Jacobs and William H. Whyte, who theorised in the 60's the need to design American houses for people rather than cars and shopping malls.

Red Location Museum of Struggle, the pergola and the porches

View of the Red Location Museum of Struggle at the beginning of the second phase. On the right, the Art Gallery under construction and the Pelip Housing

Houses and cities: the Pelipe housing

Jo Noero clearly stresses the contradictory but at the same complementary relation between the two terms 'daily' and 'extraordinary', in tune with Andrew Ballantyne (*Architecture theory: a reader in philosophy and culture*, 2005): "...*The great world is drawn in multiple ways in the local scenery.*"
Talking about daily life does not mean narrate the obviousness but what is in our sight, all that can be considered when exactly what is ordinary seems extraordinary, when apparently 'invisible' people and events represent the active and emerging figures of human dwelling. How do we explain this idea? Noero states: *"Of interest with regard to the work that I did is that my engagement was shaped through the understandings that I gained whilst studying in England in the late 1970's. The writings of John Turner were particularly important in this regard. Turner, who describes himself as an anarchist, wrote persuasively about limiting the role of the state in shaping the world within which people could choose to live – this must not be mistaken as support for the radical democracy of the unfettered market place – rather Turner argued for the state's role to be limited to ensure social justice and to be limited to those areas where people could not help themselves. I was drawn to the NGO sector precisely because it offered itself as that kind of model in which local communities acting for themselves could take charge of their everyday lives. I worked for a great number of organizations during this period who led the way in the country in the fields of housing, alternative education, cultural production and community development – in many ways I consider this period to be the most productive and creative period of my working life to date."* (Sorrell, 2009 p.9)
Here is where we can retrace the foundations of Patrick Geddes' ideas in "*Cities in Evolution*", Lewis Mumford's theories, the thoughts of Jane Jacobs, and the overcoming of urban shape in "*Life and death of great cities*", an approach focused on the (sudden) evolutions of those urban forms traditionally considered more stable.
By analysing the issues stressed by Turner in "*Housing by People*", we can see that they are still present today. Let's consider, for example, the issue of access to housing due to the increase of the urban population, the rise of social inequalities, or the fast consumption of natural resources caused by globalization and productive capitalism: in this context, it is necessary to commit to a sustainable economy. The housing issue needs to be considered in an alternative way to the exclusive '*analysis of the house's value*', from a materialistic (qualitative) and trading to a potential value.

Samanta Bartocci

Broadening the range of elements to be considered, *Red Location Cultural Precinct* looks at the tradition of self-building to foster spontaneous and responsible practices of participation. It also endorses the convivial use of spaces to support urban creativity, forms of self-organization and supports dynamic design methods as an opportunity in the urban space.
Based on these principles, *Red Location Cultural Precinct* describes the complexities and contradictions of the housing issue and, at the same time, it focuses on the possibility of providing alternative solutions to living in urban spaces heavily influenced by the ideological representation of power. Port Elizabeth is the core of the car industry in Africa, a city within the Metro Nelson Mandela metropolitan region, with more than 2.5 million inhabitants. Like all South African cities, Port Elizabeth is surrounded by townships of the apartheid era, which have been object of *'uniformity'* policies (one family, one home) in the last decades. Government interventions had the presumption of solving the housing issue. However, their consequences were rather the development of areas outside the city, and the proliferation of low-density and low-income settlements in these outskirts. Red Location was the first *'black'* settlement, founded in 1902 at the end of the Anglo-Boer war. The name derives from its buildings, iron wavy and rusted shacks of an intense red colour. Some of these were parts of a concentration camp in Uitenhage, moved to Red Location in 1900, at the end of the war. Several leading political figures – such as Goven Mbekhi, Raymond Mhlaba, George Pemba and John Kani - were born or lived in Red Location. At that time, its train station was scene of relevant passive resistance and fight events against apartheid. The majority of those historical buildings (shacks, houses) has gone through important transformations; during the years, pieces of iron were carried and re-used in other areas of the settlement.
It is possible to affirm that Red Location's houses tells us about the area's history. Today, for its importance in the *fight for equality*, it is considered an historical site together with Robben Island and Freedom Square.
Starting from the 90's already, these housing issues became central in South African's politics, when the attention turned from *the request for houses* to *housing as a need*.
The *Housing White Paper* (1994) is the first programmatic document setting the construction and assignment of residences; the *Housing Act* (1997)

View of the Red Location Museum of Struggle and the Pelip Housing

put pressure at all governmental levels in order to develop and adapt all settlements to several national standards. With the purpose of backing the interventions' quality and sustainability, as well as adopting measures to improve the *shack dwellers*'[1] housing conditions, the government launched a programme for building *"sustainable human settlements"* (2004-2009). The programme set very complex goals to solve the issue, if only for the numbers involved: 79,2% now lives in *official* houses.[2]

During the decade of *Red Location Cultural Precinct* project's development, the construction of the urban infrastructure and welfare spaces were extensively followed by protests for the delays in the housing policies' fulfilment.

The buildings foreseen in the project (a museum, archive, library, art gallery, etc.) implied the transferral of 150 families living in the shacks to new residences respecting the new housing needs, in a close-by area.

There were many protests, the constitution of committees and several consultations, following the constructions, which were divided in two long phases. In fact, through the protests, Red Location's inhabitants were able to open a channel of discussion with the municipality. The first, experimental, phase saw the birth of a small number of houses, through the *PELIP housing* project by Noero Wolffs Architects, while the second, still to be ended, filled the gap of those functional needs, widely discussed by the inhabitants with the municipality.

In this scope, the right for housing assumed strength and determination in the process, as the inhabitants fought for and got *"materially and emotionally"* involved with it, having to negotiate the housing political proposals. In fact, the housing issue recalls, on one side, the rights and welfare, while on the other represents the symbolical sector of post-apartheid policies (Montanini, 2016). This is why the project's proposals were modified during the years, eventually by Noero himself. The drafts show a different, dynamic and crowded, neighbourhood; during the XIII Venice Biennale in 2012, Jo Noero presented a huge planimetry of how Red Location had been transformed, in the vision of a *"new common territory in our city"*, explaining the possibility of the new public context, but also the possibilities of determining urban proximity and vitality through different densities and housing typologies.

Going back to the first phase, PELIP housing (1999), was financed by Port Elizabeth's municipality, in collaboration with the *Swedish International Development Agency* (SIDA). The project lies in the Eastern boundary of the broader plan for *Red Location Cultural Precinct*. The final result was 16 low budget

---

1. In reference to the dynamics of the housing policies in New Brighton, please see *Redenzione forzata; Sviluppo, post-apartheid e pratiche di appropriazione a Red Location*, M. Montanini (2016-17), PhD in Social and Political Change, XXIX cycle.
2. StaSa, Community Census, 2016.

houses conceived by Noero Wolff Architects as innovative devices, able to demonstrate the values and possibilities of self-determination and adaptation. It was important that the inhabitants understood how the houses could improve their wellness and general living standards. The project used low-budget materials, of course, but the value of a decent home is given especially by the inversion of the paradigm by which a single RDP house[3] becomes a small *high-density housing* unit. These 4x20 meters building plots were finally coupled to form two-family homes. Building two-family homes with 2 or 3 floors means providing a great house that can be extended both in the front and in the back side.

Space for the community is the implicit idea of PELIP houses. The buildings host business activities at the ground floor and homes on the upper floors. The spaces were assigned to different segments of population, from the young to the elder, and families with handicapped persons. In order to question the government's conventional[4] approach, it was necessary to define principles, alternatives and choices able to change the perception and the debate on the construction industry, by fostering the predisposition for users' diversification, better income conditions and a greater care for the environment (including the use of local materials and the preservation of water). Noero states that this approach *"doesn't solve all the housing issues but is only one of the numerous initiatives that should be launched"*. With this in mind, PELIP Housing Company realized different housing projects in the same area, emblematic of the housing various declinations.

PELIP houses raises the housing issue in terms of public microcredit; designs buildings that can accommodate the greatest spectrum of inhabitant needs; creates jobs and provides new skills to the population. A good housing project abides the issues of sustainability, and contributes to balancing the values between the average population density and the progressive occupation of territories. This consideration is fundamental in *"South Africa today where the continued outward expansion of cities driven by current housing policy is creating unsustainable communities far from work opportunities and the other amenities that people need to sustain a reasonable urban life. The self help model is only one of many models which can be employed in low-income housing. There is a role for the designed medium density and formally constructed process"*.[5]

---

3. Among the decisions set by the *Housing White Paper*, the *Reconstruction and Development Programme* (RDP) was promoted by the African National Congress (ANC), led by Nelson Mandela in 1994. This comprehensive plan foresaw the construction of 300.000 houses in 5 years, setting the targets of growth, development and reducing poverty.
4. The historical legacy of apartheid is the image of a city made of houses, families and plots of land in neighbourhoods which look all alike. An approach considered unsustainable, debilitating and anti-urban.
5. https://divisare.com/projects/173702-noero-wolff-architects-pelip-housing

**Site plan and section of the Red Location
Cultural Precinct and the social houses (Ongoing)**

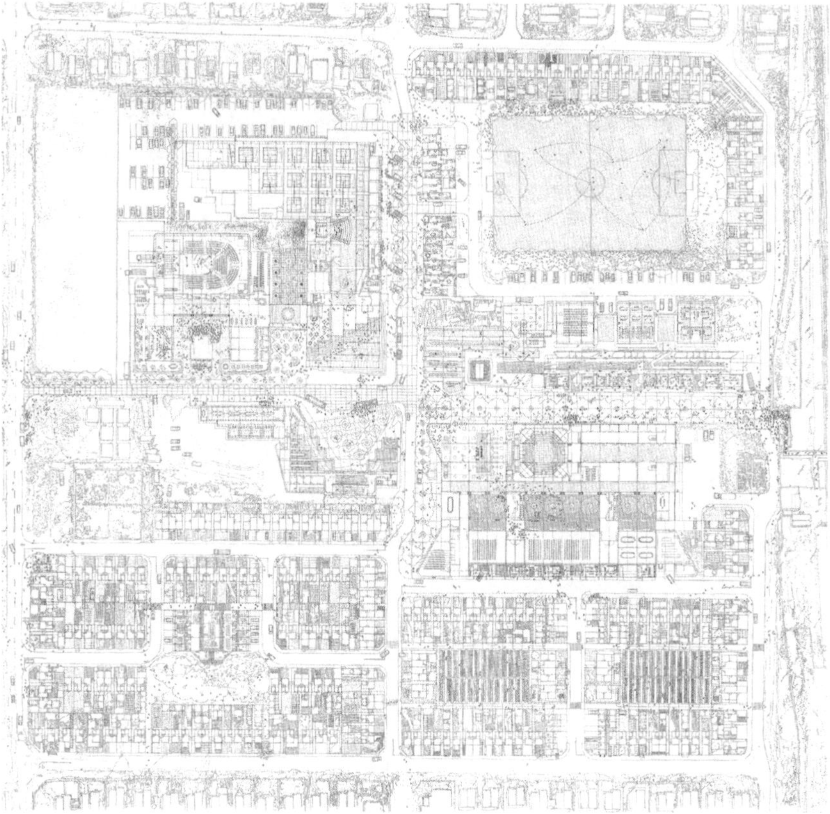

View of the Museum of Struggle from the Pelip Housing entrance

**Pelip Housing (1999), from top right,
the typological approaches, plan and elevation**

A project focusing on the process rather than the final product, in spite of the context's complexities, suggests the possibility of its re-proposition. By acknowledging the opportunity of building elsewhere, we need to observe the local (social, cultural, environmental, etc.) conditions first, and allow the polysemous value of diversification to emerge, bearing in mind the importance of creating a context to take care of and enhancing the richness of its everyday life.

"Good, thoughtful design could make in achieving a better life for all. This is not to suggest that a well-designed house will solve the problems of equity in a highly unequal society. However, to us architects involved in the field of housing it's clear that a well-designed home can make all the difference to a family in as much as it can become a vehicle for better health, capital growth and investment and can also become the social and cultural centre of a vital family life". (Noero 1999)

Detail of east elevation showing the concrete block construction, with corrugated tin and some stucco, and the wide public porch along the pedestrian street

© noero architects archives

**Study of site plan and elevation,
for the proposal of social housing (ongoing)**

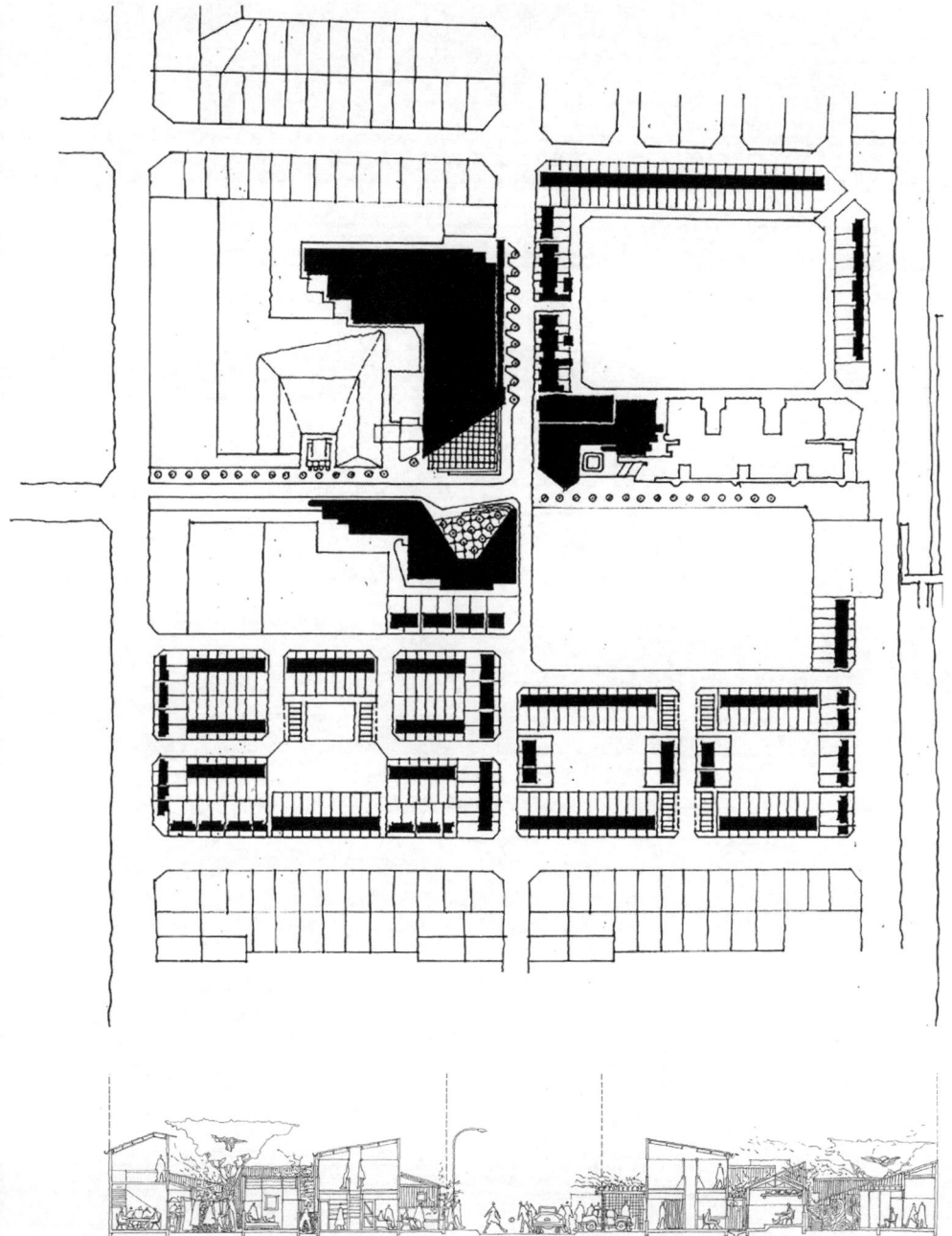

The urban space between the Museum of the Struggle and Pelip Housing

© noero architects archives

Memory box: *the Museum of Struggle*

In *"Archaeology of Knowledge"* (1969), Foucault challenged the one-directional, scientific knowledge structure linked to a single power, asking the question: *"which are the the mechanisms underlying the development of knowledge?"* Foucault observes as well how the focus of attention for historians had shifted from the large periods of time, such as *eras* or *centuries*, to the *events of change*. In this view, the problem is not to retrace solid traditions *"but fractures and limits, not of the perpetual foundations anymore, but of those transformations which can represent the foundations and the foundation's renovation"*. This statement has entailed several consequences. In first place prevails the *"surface effect"*, namely the increasing number of fractures in the history of human thought reaching the surface; the proposed method implies the impossibility of identifying a linear chain of causes to define a link between the facts. *"Disparities and waste in every day's life scenarios prevail"*. (Marotta, 2015) We have to face, instead, a series of events that have to be defined one by one, with their limits and relations, abandoning the reason's chronology, which develops and is produced in a linear way, recalling the differences in planning and the multitude of meanings. It would mean to adopt an *operational concept*, one of *"discontinuity"*, which selects the different fields of study and *"delimits the scope of the effect's action"*. *The transformational post-colonial South African city* (Morell 2011) has that particular inclination to emphasize the urban dynamics of *experienced* urban spaces, those in which you can feel *"underground life and disobedience to rules"*. The *Red Location Museum of Struggle* (1998-2005) is among this category of places because it tells us about a discontinuity and a physical description of living conditions during apartheid, invoking cultural memories rather than history.

The building is paradigmatic of post-apartheid, post-colonial architecture. Noero Wolff Architecture's studio decided to *"represent a non-linear vision of history, like a mix of memories linked to each other but consciously disconnected"*. (Morell, 2011)

Red Location's spatial fractures reveal like an enquiry for change. The Museum of Struggle is only a part of New Brighton's broad redevelopment; however, Noero underlines the fact that *"monuments depicting great scenes of victory usually cause a feeling of bitterness among the population, once it has moved on"*.

Samanta Bartocci

From this point of view, the architects decided to adopt the approach of a multi-level project to mark the modifications of space, experience after experience, project after project. Their goal is to affirm the principle of an ongoing process, a constant mutation: the idea of a *permanent revolution*.
In the heart of New Brighton, among the unusual tangles of rusted shacks, the projects and buildings linked to the Museum integrate respectfully and harmonically the cultural and physical fabric. After many attempts to divert the funding to other projects in the city, finally the municipality start the Museum's construction. This building was intentionally conceived to challenge the memorial Museum's conventional vision. Memory is not sufficient; we need the representation of daily life and to overturn the concept that *"the mind's structure needs to remember, in order to protect itself from experiences, and has to forget, to maintain the system in balance"*. (Marotta, 2015)

"Jo Noero, paraphrasing Andreas Huyssen, writes "we should move beyond the museum's present role as a giver of canonical truths and cultural authority, duping its visitors as manipulated and reified cultural cattle." This is clearly a reference to the curatorial and spatial strategy adopted by museums like the Holocaust and the Gold Reef Apartheid Museums, where a single narrative strain is coordinated with space, light, movement, texture and sound to instill in the viewer, through the physical power of architecture, a simulation of bodily experience". (Findley, 2013)
The project is based on Andreas Huyssen's work of historian and critic. The museum confronts itself with the concept of museum indeed as a space for interaction and freedom, especially addressed to those who were denied this right denied. For this reason, the museum's external space was realized to host multiple solutions, flexible and adaptable to the population's future needs, and is part of a broader urban structure. The interior as well is not organized to be an obligatory path but as a space free to walk through, with objects exposed all around.
The Museum of Struggle's undifferentiated space houses a *"plastic fact"*, a *Memory Box* device, a box filled of goods and emotional experiences, a *cognitive assembly* (Le Doux, 2016) of those migrant workers divided and eradicated from their families. These artefacts are decorated in different ways and represent the numerous cultural and religious South African realities; however, they actually are reproductions of private spaces *"filled with public purposes"*.

**Entrance view of the Red Location
Museum of Struggle; Phase 1**

© noero architects archives

Design sketch of the plan of the Red Location Cultural Precinct

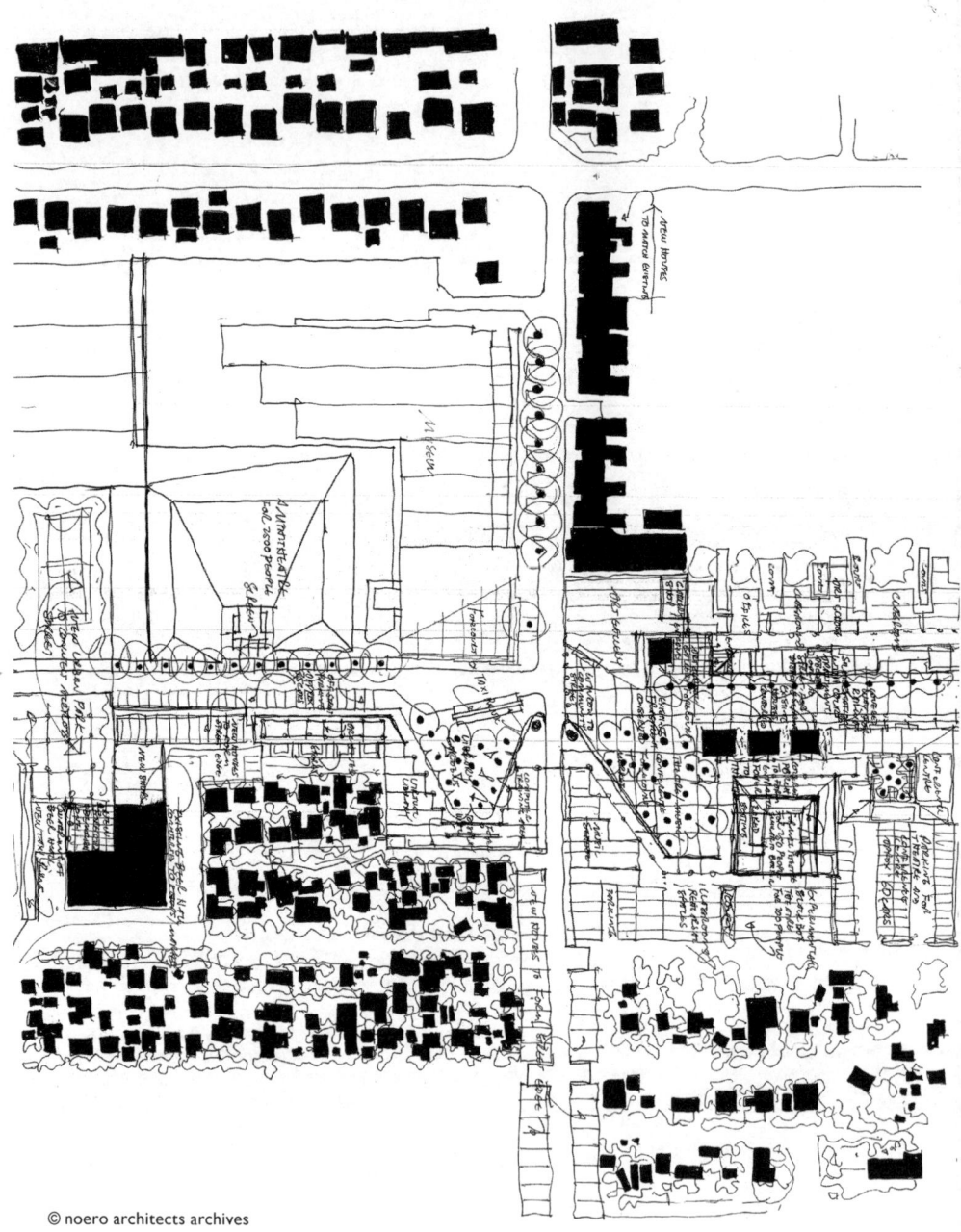

© noero architects archives

The road from the former barracks to the Museum of Struggle

These 12 boxes are 6m wide, 6m long and almost 12m tall; they are arranged geometrically, thought to be the main attraction. These boxes contain rusted, silent amnesias and memories, eroded by space and the experience of helplessness; in silence, they expose the absolute value of life, while their content is secret. "*There is no sequence: the content and subjects are deliberately juxtaposed, for a full experience in every box*". Between the boxes there is space for reflection and present time. Huyssen named this the *memory's double light*, a crepuscular light holding both dreams and reality. Inside the museum's area we can also find an auditorium, an art gallery, offices and a

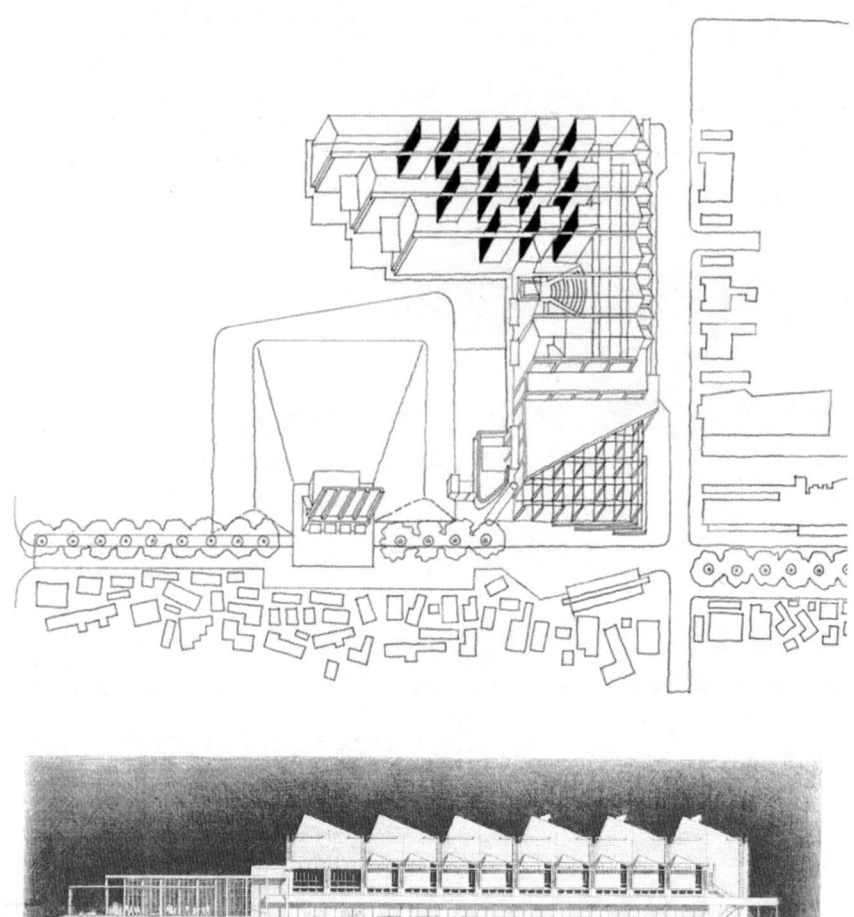

Sketch of the first phase of the project of Museum of Struggle; the main museum and gallery space showing memory boxes, and the great green space outside

memorial for the national heroes, including the graves of Raymond Mhlaba and Goven Beki. The entrance is a huge covered walkway covered by a wooden harbour, marking the building's entrance but also a broader space of interaction opening towards the playground, able to welcome large demonstrations. The eastern side of the building is therefore transformed in an *inhabitable* wall with seats, the playground and parking for taxi.
The idea of freeing space is part of Noero's critical research, referred to the theories described by Allison and Peter Smith in *Ordinariness and Light*. The concept was to create a kind of architecture serving as a *scaffolding* for daily life, in order to recognize and realise its new being.

Memory boxes as devices of memory, amnesia, and space of experience of apartheid and South African culture

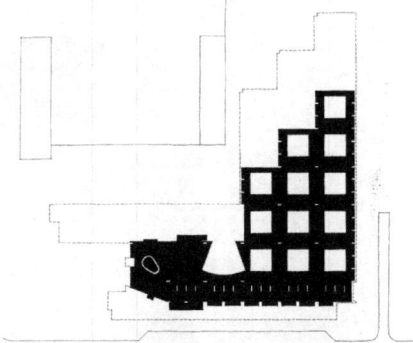

© noero architects archives

A first elaboration of the exhibition space

Coupled to this concept of space is the authors' choice for that informal materialism inspired from local traditions. Through a combination of principles, the project marks a fracture with the European's tradition in monumental museums aesthetics. The territory in which lies the *Cultural Precinct* is lived precisely as Lefebvre defines daily life: contradictory, unstable and unpredictable. In this process of structure creation in space, the museum's building strategy and use of local materials are essential for the architecture's invention.
Pushed by this strong belief, Noero worked *effectively with Mandela's city officials to adjust and negotiate their expectations on the project with the community's desires.* At the same time, New Brighton's community organized committees in charge of monitoring the work's progress at all planning and building stages, which were necessary to assure, in the first place, the protection of the project's residences and accompanying infrastructures, and, in the second place, the employment of local labour, allowing the company to modify prices and construction plans.

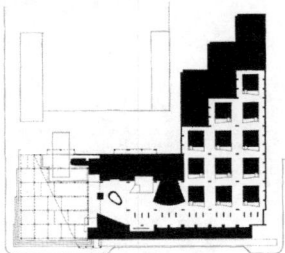

Light study drawing for main gallery. The museum section and the saw-tooth factory image

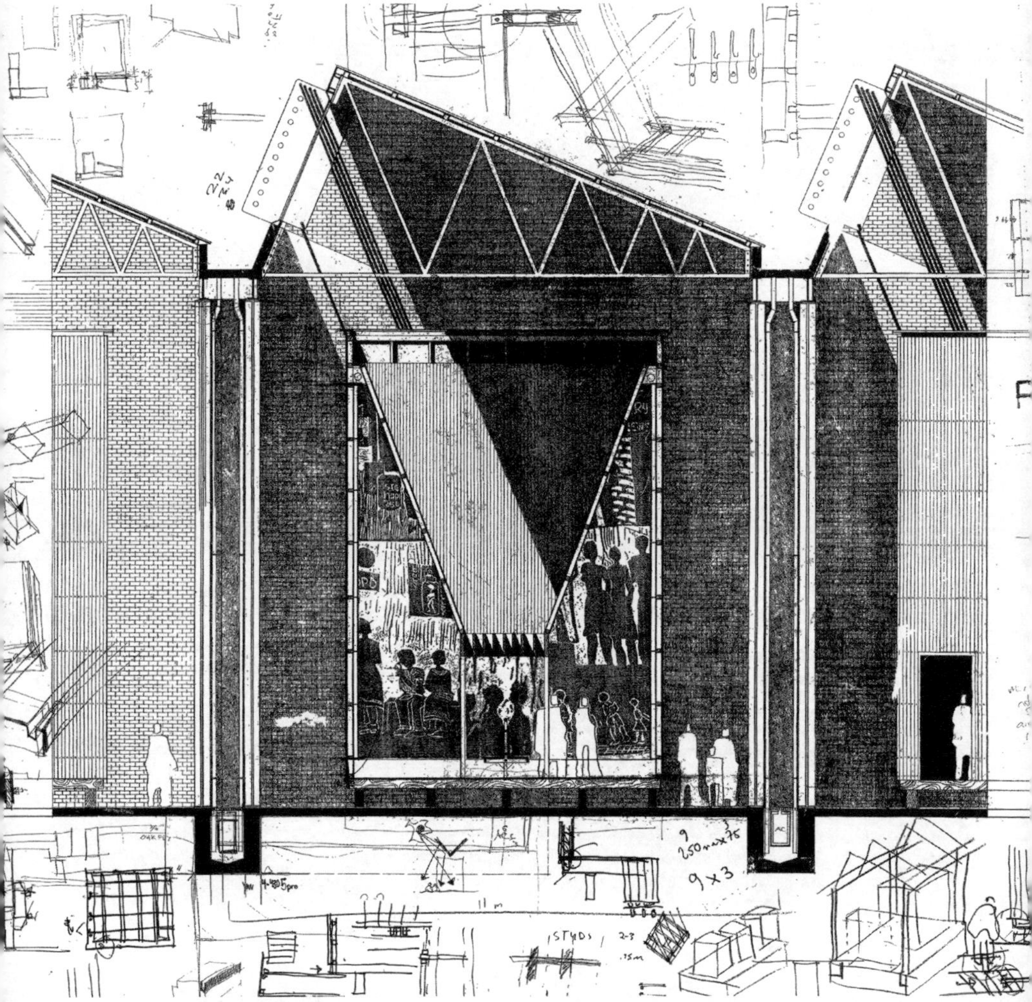

The contemplative space at the exterior of the memory box

© noero architects archives

The exhibit hall of the Museum.

Sections of the Post-Apartheid Museum

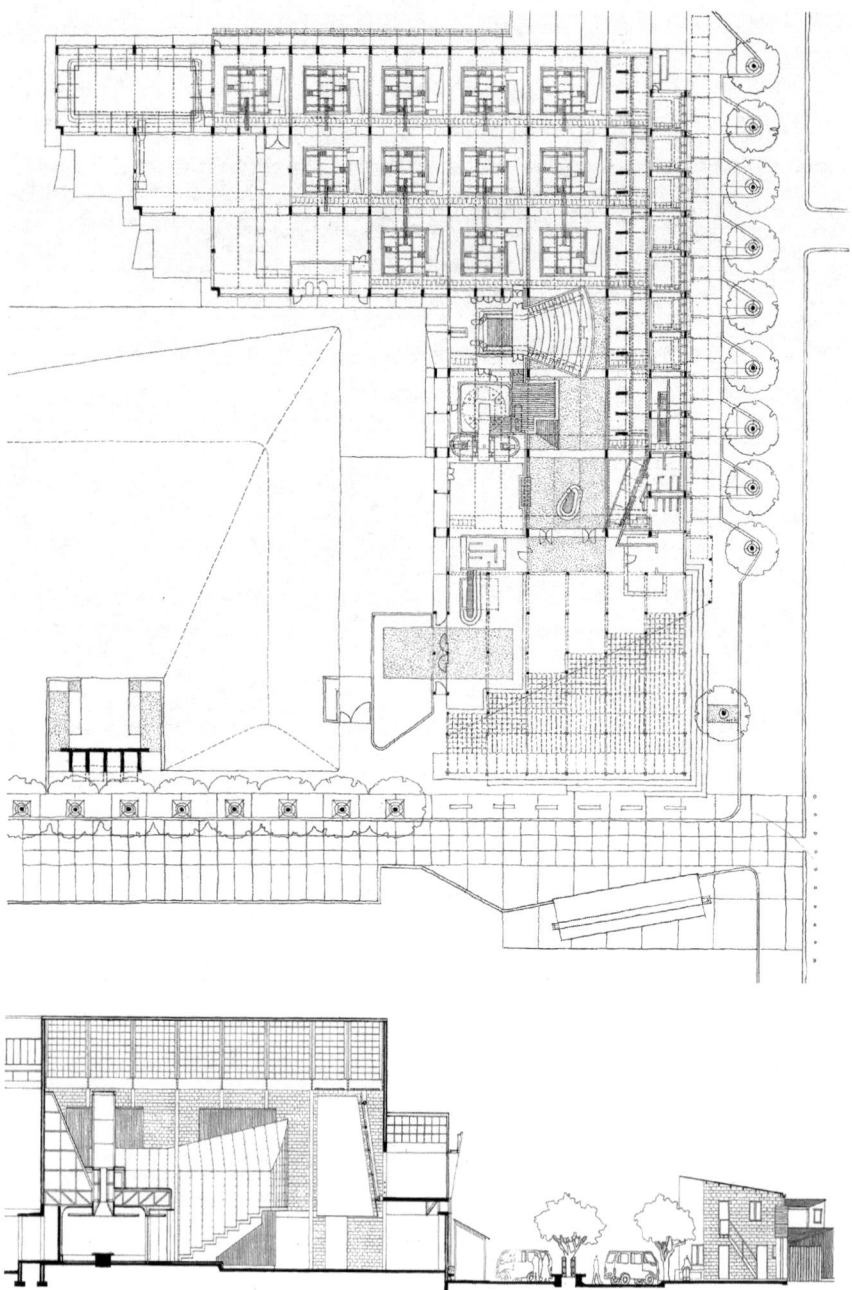

The plan and the museum section elevation, and the auditorium

The exhibition space

The project's contract includes the provision of employing 50% of labour among unskilled inhabitants, following a rotation policy of 90 days. The construction period was delayed to 18 months. 540 workers chosen among the local population were involved in the Museum's construction.

The museum establishes a comfortable relation with its extensions – the covered walkway, the shadowed paths, the recesses, stairs, ramps and open green spaces – which modulate the spatial compressions and expansions in order to allow the ordinary structures to become public space.

New Brighton's landscape, characterized by architecturally poor factories and an important train station, lived the civic dimension of *"monumental production"*. The topic of memory comes back, and after all it can't be replaced by justice... *"Memory is always transitory, notoriously unreliable, and haunted by forgetting – in short, human and social. As public memory it is subject to change: political, generational, individual. It cannot be stored forever, nor can it be secured by monuments; nor, for that matter, can we rely on digital retrieval systems to guarantee coherence and continuity. If the sense of lived time is being renegotiated in our contemporary cultures of memory, we should not forget that time is not only the past, its preservation and transmission. If we are indeed suffering from a surfeit of memory, we do need to make the effort to distinguish usable pasts from disposable pasts.Discrimination and productive remembering are called for, and mass culture and the virtual media are not inherently irreconcilable with that purpose. Even if amnesia were a by-product of cyberspace, we must not allow the fear of forgetting to overwhelm us. And then perhaps it is time to remember the future, rather than only worry about the future of memory".* (Huyssen, 2000)

The auditorium

© noero architects archives

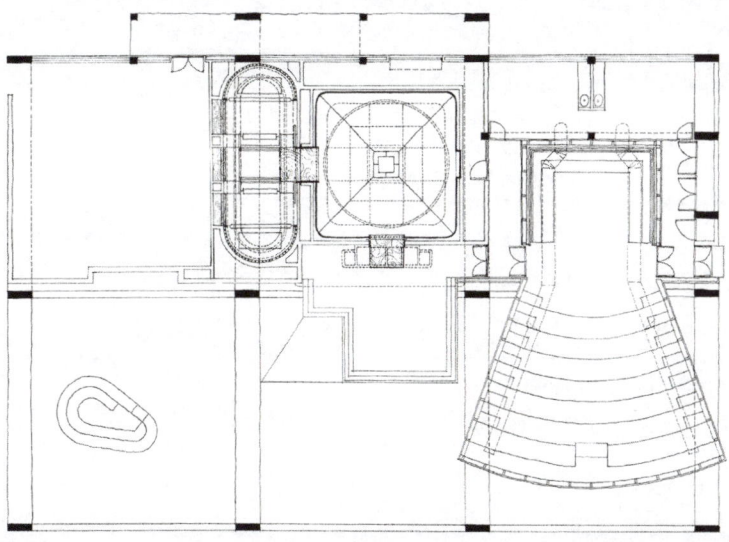

The inner space of the museum of Struggle and the entrance to the auditorium

External view from the playgrounds; phase 1

© noero architects archives

Living space:
The library, archive and art gallery

Spaces of interaction
"Architecture can open minds, and can find new ways to reunite them" (Melvin, 2011). This statement by Jo Noero brings back the urban space to be an important asset in the project, and to be the place providing the coordinates to build *ways and worlds to live together*. In this sense, the availability and openness of space are essential to build a space for each and every one.
Red Location Cultural Precinct's project is based on the research of these principles, sustaining the '*public*' dimension, from the local level to the wider context of Nelson Mandela's city municipality.

The first supporters of a cultural area in Red Location's context, and its consequent transformation, were the local counsellor Jimmy Tutu and, in particular, Rory Riordan, the district project manager, economist and former director of Human Rights Trust.
Their idea was to follow the concept of cultural district as a means for the territory's development, in great contrast with the socio-economic policies adopted in other areas of the city, and more generally all over the country.
In *Red Location Cultural Precinct*, Noero moves away the concept of production and consumption unit. On the contrary, he aims to rediscover the concepts of necessity and repossession, paying particular attention to the ways in which architecture becomes a support to the human dimension. It is possible to develop a city like an urban operating system in every place (Maciocco, 2011), but this system shall contain the typical differential quality of spaces, which creates the positive ambiguity of marginality, and supports us in recognizing all the different shapes in which contemporary human condition is expressed.
On several occasions Noero, while reflecting on the African urban dimension[1], clearly states how strong is the influence of Europe in the projects for the South African cities. In first place, the public spaces as political spots (for example, the traditional representation of political power), has little value in the South African cities. However, it is more appropriate to consider the experience of the *otherness* as an intimate vocation of the

---
1. South African urbanization begins with the mines and is historically influenced by migrations. In its modern expressions, urbanization is a mix of the African and European worlds.

Samanta Bartocci

space of roads. In South African cities, the road turns to be a space with potential, home to numerous formal and informal activities; a limited but real form of direct democracy, of informal self-government.
In Red Location, roads are the starting point of the public space's development. Public life is expressed in the roads. Today's *Olaf Palme Avenue* and *Avenue C* are the roads that historically connected the railway bridge to *Deal Party*'s factories. In those same roads, the inhabitants protested in name of *freedom*; these roads are true space-time landmarks.
Red Location's project didn't focus on being a vast public space, but rather to be accurately structured as an *open* one.
Red Location's project is structured in different architectural elements: the Museum, opened to public in November 2006[2]; the playground; the new road paving, and the PELIP housing[3] eastern front. During a second construction phase, the library, archive and art gallery, all spaces for learning, were realized, besides all the small public spaces associated to the main roads (benches, platform roofs and trees). This construction phase ended in 2011[4]. The following ones foresee the building of 210 social housing units, an arts and crafts school, a back-packers lodge, and a commercial area for a supermarket and other business activities.
Red Location is an expression of post-apartheid freedom, and an opportunity for social experience. After 43 years of segregation, Red Location represents the possibility to move freely in the public space.
All the buildings realized during these two phases, "move" in space, in the barely perceived dilatation between the road and the square. These intermediate spaces within the public and the building represent a possibility of approach, an opportunity for social interaction.

2. The Red Location Museum's design was presented during an exhibition at the MOMA New York in 2010.
3. The project for the contest and the first constructing phase are fruit of Noero Wolff Architects' work (Jo Noero [Principal] and Heinrich Wolff), in association with John Blair Architect.
4. Beginning from this phase, the Art Gallery, Library and Archive projects were designed by Jo Noero [Principle] and Robert McGiven, in association with John Blair Architect; Noero Wolff Architects has been dissolved. The future work for Red Location will be carried out by Noero Architects.

The Art Gallery

Red Location Cultural Precinct
1 Museum (phase 1)
2 PELIP housing(phase 1)
3 Art Gallery (phase 2)
4 Digital Library and Archive (phase 2)

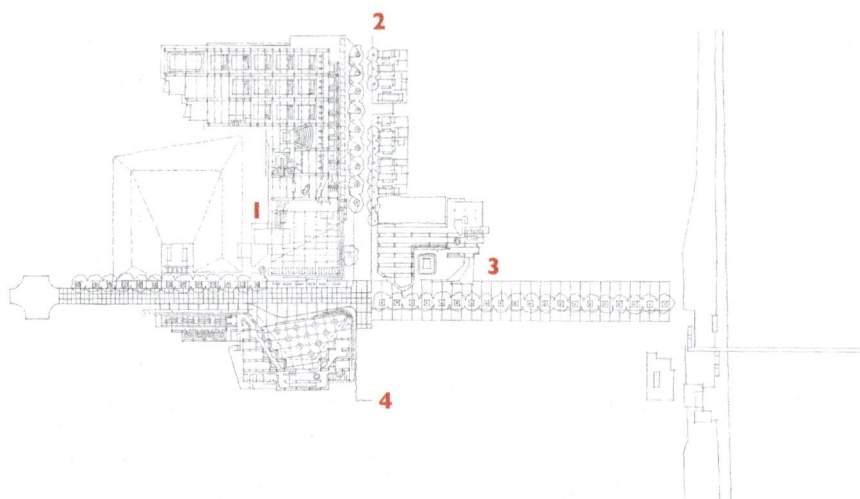

The new art gallery is located on the North side, next to the Skyman's Supermarket (then transformed into a pension), and digs a U-shape courtyard in order to enclose an original house in wavy iron of 1902[5]. Quite a vestige of resistance or a reminder of that inhumanity. "*The shack installation, or 'imitation' as described by du Preez, 'was done deliberately to divert foreign tourists looking for an "authentic" experience, from constantly invading the privacy of people's homes opposite the museum. 'The 'imitation' shack provides 'an "authentic" experience' that diverts attention away from 'people's homes'*" (Smith, 2016). This object's interpretation provokes conflicting opinions, as well as the entire operation of the context's transformation. The presence of the isolated house brings us back to the local everyday life and, at the same time, allows us to retrace the urban stratifications, just like an

---

5. In 1902, during the Anglo-Boer war, approximately 800 iron and wooden houses and barracks were dismantled and used to build the Uitenhage concentration camp and an hospital. They were eventually transferred to Red Location. Today, it is probably the oldest occupied "*Location*" in South Africa. In the 20th century, while the political militancy increased, deterioration, lack of water and electricity, as well as insufficient hygiene, made life conditions even worse. In more than 100 years since their reassembling, Red Location's building were continuously repaired, adjusted and recycled.

The Art Gallery and the last building in wood and iron by Red Location. "Red" for the red oxide paint used to protect the corrugated metal of New Brighton's homes

© noero architects archives

archaeological site. Eroded by time, badly designed, inhabitable and useless, but still an expression of daily life.
Surrounding the house, the precinct's wall, and the gallery's volumetric and spatial development in particular, are specifically aimed to express this external area's *'porosity'*, more and more available to embrace non codified practices.
Inside, at the centre of the gallery towards Olaf Palme Avenue, the space is closed. It was built to host multimedia events. Reinforcing the concept of threshold, in the entrance fold, a huge glass separates it from the outside. The goal is to *showcase* a section of the gallery, enhancing the polyvalent use of the exhibition space, which was designed to support the local artists and, in particular, to promote internationalisation in the permanent exhibition named *Eastern Cape Struggle Art*[6]
Although small, this space has all the safety measures to host international exhibitions. Moreover, the buildings' orientation (south) was an important feature in order to modulate the sunshine's light on the horizontal surfaces. As in the museum, the art gallery, the library and the archive, space is generous, both in the inside and the outside, in spite of its complexity. They were all built with a very low budget, thanks to the architect's ability to hire the local population.
In this scope, Noero took advantage of its skills, not only on the construc-

The Art Gallery exybition space, plan and section

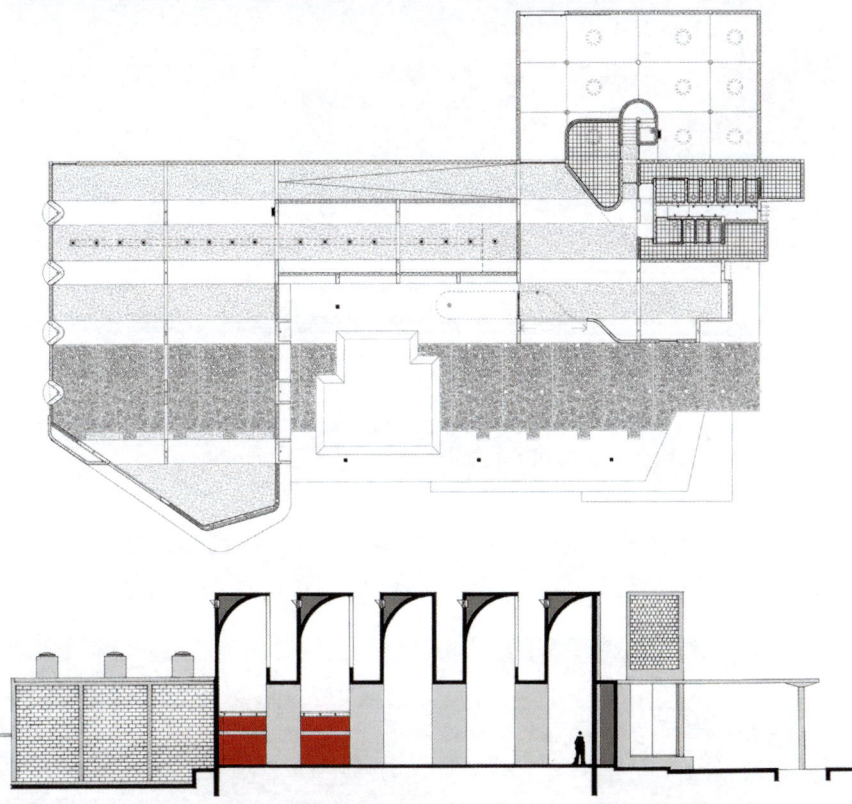

tion site but also, and especially, for the project. For example, the archive's upholstery was conceived in *Tsitsikamma* wood, traditionally used for its low cost and robustness to build enclosures and animal shelters, and locally abundant. This wood, treated to resist adverse weather conditions, eventually turns into a greyish colour, very similar to other kinds of wood used for building houses in the area. The archive's interior is also covered with this material, a huge, long and thin wooden box[7], enlightened by a striped skylight. The archive, located in parallel to *Olaf Palm Avenue*, is the tallest building in the district. From this point, a thin concrete platform roof stretches out towards the library running along the road. In this case as well, the edge was modelled to obtain seating capacity. To get to the

---

6. The Ernest Cole Photographic Exhibition was the first to be held, in June 2011, by the Hasselblad Foundation from Sweden.
7. The lecture room built on two level hosts a precious collection of books about the city's struggle, and the famous Afrikaner's one.

The hall and spaces for temporary exhibitions

© noero architects archives

Entrance of the library and the archive

© noero architects archives

**The Archive and library comprises
a digital library and internet café computer school**

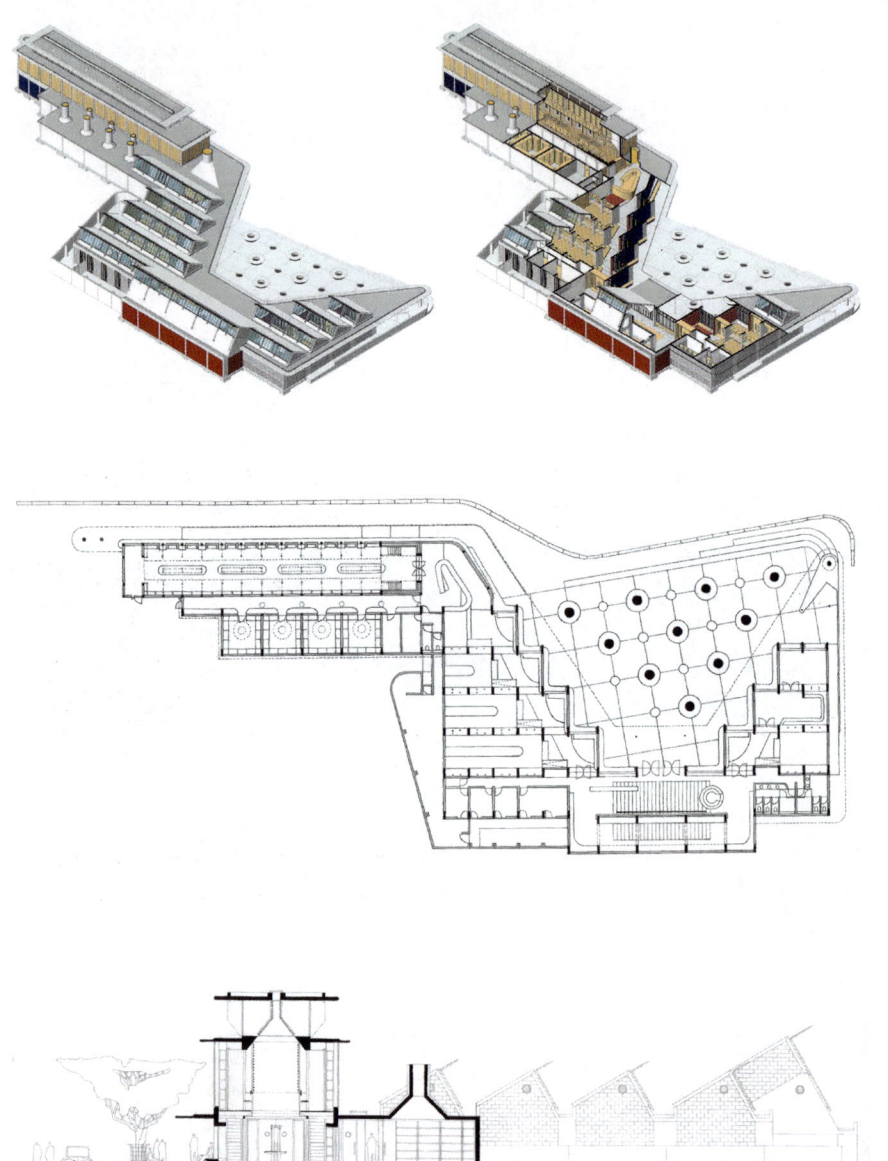

The library

The entrance hall of the library and the kinshasa tapestry, Keiskamma Guernica (2010)

The archive

The library and Archive and the Museum of Stuggle, elevation

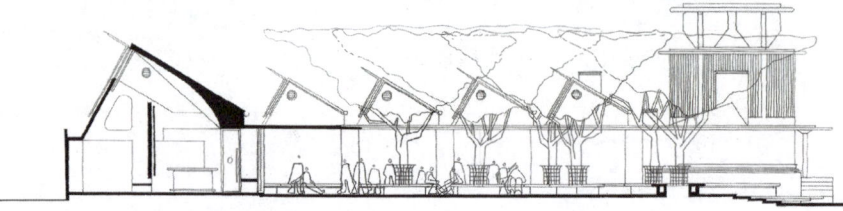

The library and Archive (phase 2)

archive it is necessary to walk through the digital library, whose entrance is facing a large square ending with a wide platform roof.
The roof's covering contains the both the books of the library and the archive. The same structure used for the museum (a section made of shed covers) allows, also in this case, the natural light to enter the reading and working areas; all buildings are provided of efficient heating systems and get naturally refreshed, allowing to satisfy all comfort needs without using air conditioning.
The entrance hall was designed to host a 9 by 3.5 meters tapestry, representing a *Guernica* by Picasso. Embroidered by women from the near town of Motherwell, it tells us the story of those among them who died of HIV. With the tapestry, these women express their moral commitment to democratic and civil values. Space interprets, both inside and outside, the

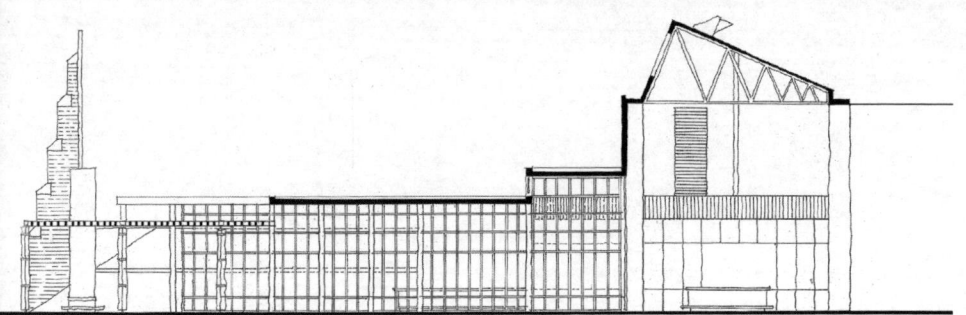

people's educational needs and their need for differentiation. Therefore, in this experimental context in which knowledge is based on experience rather than formal education (schools), Noero let the space become the element through which the learning process occurs.

Explicitly following Aldo Van Eyck's work, the library's floor was designed to obtain more rooms inside on roo, and therefore to enhance the library's widespread space, exactly because it's made of smaller ones.

The use of space in Red Location is, therefore, the first thing that changes; it suggests the idea of a new form of urbanism, open to any kind of social interaction. Contrary to all forms of functional determinism, this process enables the users to take over space, changing their role from simple *'users'* to *'inhabitants'*. Finally, these practical opportunities promote interaction in many ways, raising the space to positions of reciprocal relation, as in a diagram, a sort of operational device whose potential can be developed.

The process began in 1994, with the proposal, followed by the architectural competition in 1998, to develop Red Location into a cultural district. It experienced moments of financial and social difficulty, causing the works to stop in several occasions[8], and putting a strain on those parts of buildings already realized (the second construction phase ended in 2011). In spite of this, the municipality never stopped raising funds to complete *Red Location Cultural Precinct*, expecting a third phase of construction (two theatres with 1000 and 400 seats, a cinema, two rehearsal rooms, a school of art with rooms for workshops and laboratories, and 210 houses with two floors).

---

8. The museum was occupied by the locals for a few years. Symbolically, they became the owners of the public space. This was due to financial and operational delays in the construction of social houses for 150 displaced families.

The archive and library, entrance

© noero architects archives

Spaces of representation: different worlds

In the background
How can an idea survive to its translation and become a powerful expression in a completely different context? (Noero, 2012)
Noero questions himself on the value of projects as mere transpositions of the individual/designer's values and practices, even when these derive from the same collective culture; and on projects as a set of devices going beyond their spatial value.
The practice of architect entails the conscious inclusion of practices coming from different places and cultures. They are then re-elaborated and transformed by the project, which converts them into rich, lavish and attractive spaces, eradicated in different contexts.
The project for Red Location aims to give an answer to these questions, and it does it by dwelling on the meaning of complexity. The word 'complex' derives from the latin 'cum' and 'plectere' (weaved together), and refers to *all phenomenon, process and problem with twines; that can't be explained, but can only be understood by creating a structure of relations which connects them inextricably to other contexts and environments* (Tagliagambe, 2016). The more a system is complex, the more we need tools that can help us orient in it. These tools are not able to reproduce reality in an *accurate* way. For example, if we consider a *map*[1], we can't say it represents the territory, because all maps reproduce it inaccurately (Tagliagambe, 2016).
In a similar way, the use of metaphors, images, or suggestions, able of indicating a specific relation between map and territory, mark the end of the boundaries so that they become the reality. In *Eudoxia*, one of Calvino's *Invisible Cities*, "*at first sight nothing seems to resemble Eudoxia less than the design of that carpet, laid out in symmetrical motives whose patterns are repeated along straight and circular lines, interwoven with brilliantly colored spires, in a*

---

1. *Sylvie and Bruno* (1893), Lewis Carroll's last novel, might be interesting to read to have an insight on how a model adapts to a city, and what it entails: "*That's another thing we've learned from your Nation,*" said Mein Herr, "*map-making. But we've carried it much further than you. What do you consider the largest map that would be really useful?*"..."*About six inches to the mile.*"..."*Only six inches!*"exclaimed Mein Herr. "We very soon got to six yards to the mile. Then we tried a hundred yards to the mile. And then came the grandest idea of all! We actually made a map of the country, on the scale of a mile to the mile!*"..."*Have you used it much?*" I enquired."*It has never been spread out, yet,*" said Mein Herr: "*the farmers objected: they said it would cover the whole country, and shut out the sunlight! So we now use the country itself, as its own map, and I assure you it does nearly as well.*"

Samanta Bartocci

The Theatres (phase 3)

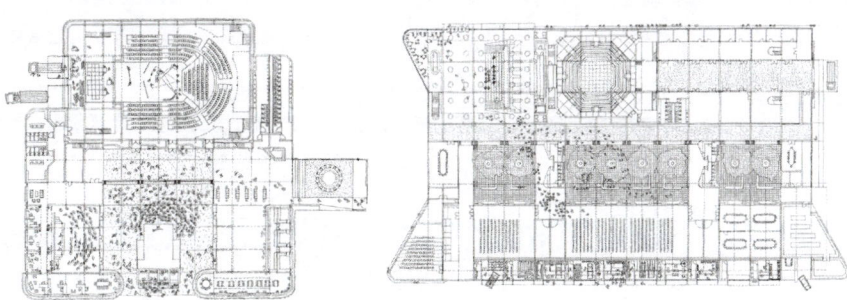

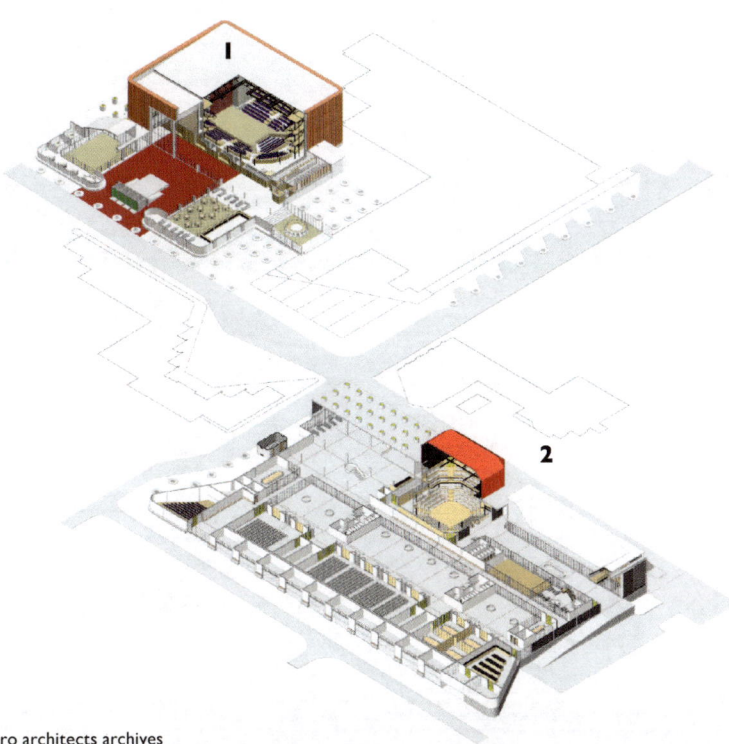

© noero architects archives

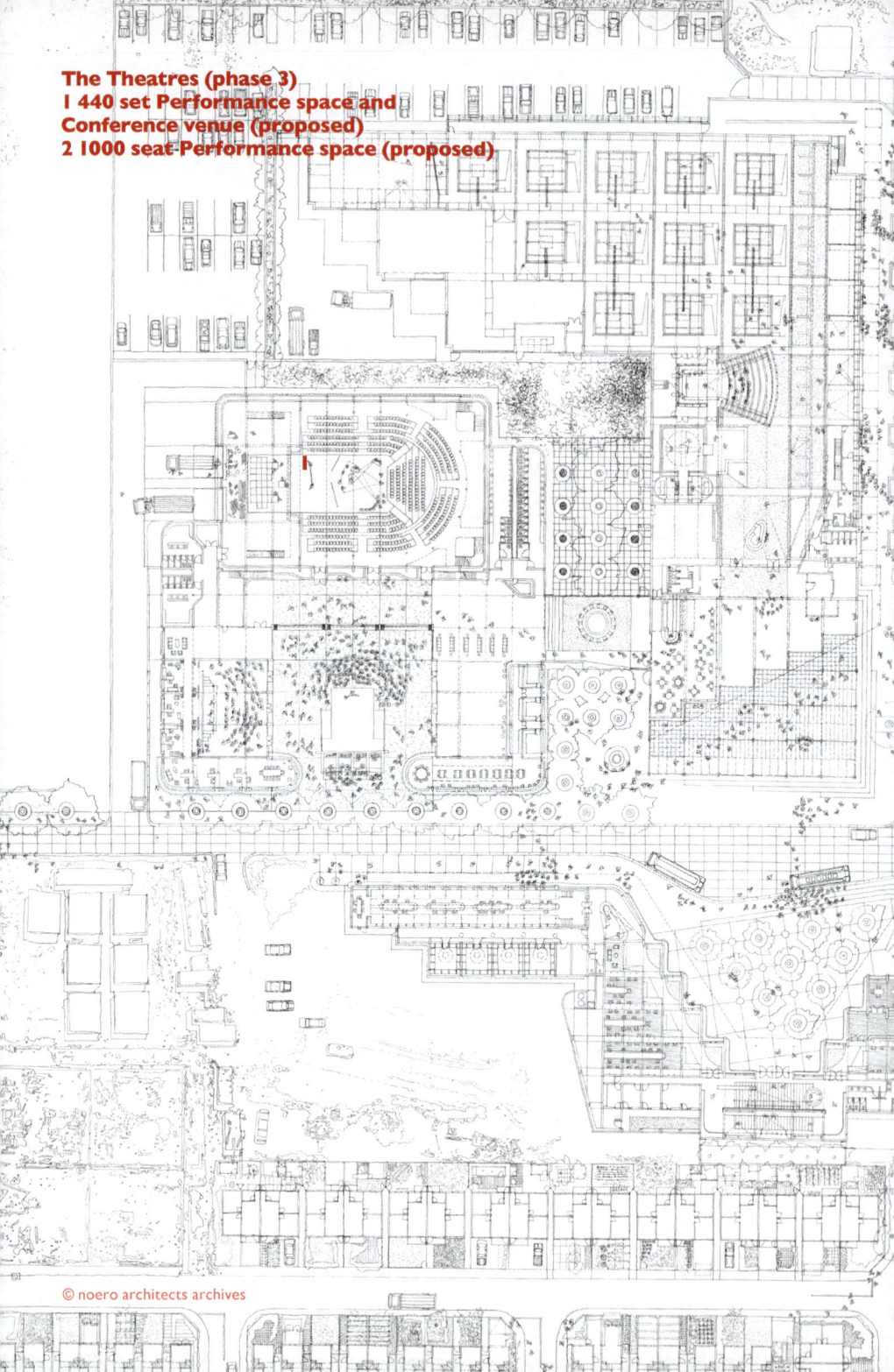

The Theatres (phase 3)
1 440 set Performance space and Conference venue (proposed)
2 1000 seat Performance space (proposed)

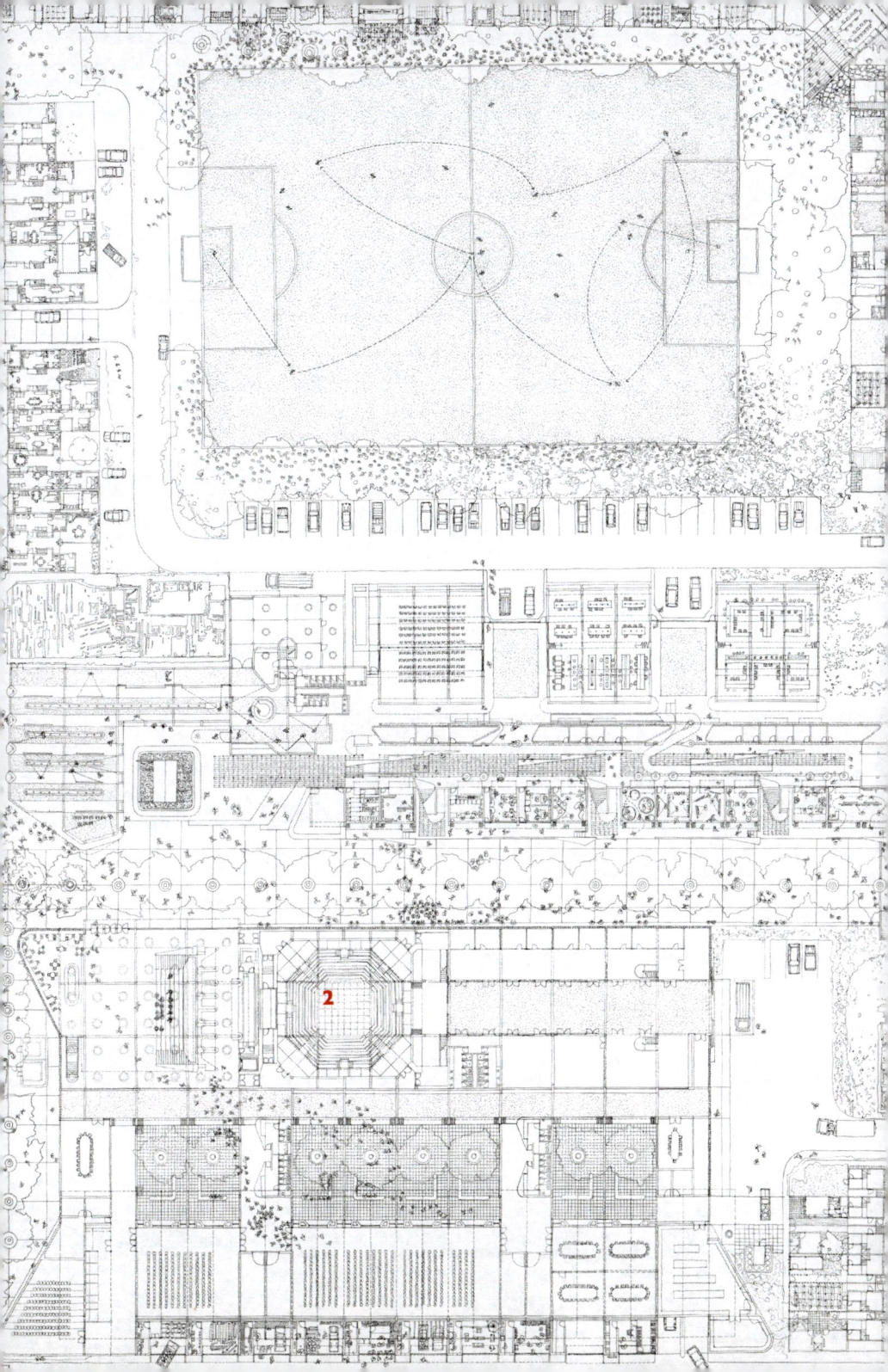

Red Location "2025 Design" (phase 3)

repetition that can be followed throughout the whole woof. But if you pause and examine it carefully, you become convinced that city and all the things contained in the city are included in the design, arranged according to their true relationship, which escapes your eye distracted by the bustle, the trongs, the shoving."[2]
The city can therefore communicate through the *carpet*, but the *carpet* cannot narrate the city, it can *explain* it (Maciocco, Tagliagambe, 1999), it replies if questioned, and helps the city not to lose orientation. It is interesting, and rather complex, to understand the underlying relation between map and territory[3], carpet and city, these two *'mysterious objects'*. For sure, metaphors represent in some way the necessary combination to understand and connect different experiences.
Aware of the map's 'inaccuracy', and of its selective experience, Noero explains again through architecture, while presenting *"Transformation of Red Location"* at the XIII Biennale of Venice (2012), the need to have a vision expressing the duality of time: *"chronological and atmospheric"*, as defined by A. Rossi. We can't know the world by representing it, we can rather design it considering in the background the dual nature of time, that recalls life in its process and its consumption. In this way, the indivisible variety of instruments on the map convert into operational tools.
The attempt to identify the tools and will to trace a common ground between city and architecture, architecture and daily life[4], was expressed at the 13th edition of the Biennale, directed by Chipperfield, and named *"Common Ground, what we have in common"*. Noero addresses this issue exposing his meticulous work on two panels of a dual nature: on the first, a huge hand-made tapestry by the Keiskamma Women's Project from

---

2. *Eudoxia, Invisible Cities*, I. Calvino, Helen and Kurt Wolff Books, London 1978, p.96.
3. This relation is well described in G. Maciocco and S. Tagliagambe (1997), *La città possibile, territorialità e comunicazione nel progetto urbano*. The city as continuous social construction is a possible city, in which *"technical knowledge and common sense intersect in the quest for a common ground"*.
4. The same subject was picked up by Aravena in 2016, with an attempt to connect the world of architecture with the participants involved.
5. Noero has been working on this project for the last 15 years, and will continue doing so. It is a very low-budget project, with the great intention of building a settlement characterized by public spaces in a forgotten district of Port Elizabeth, devastated by apartheid. In his work, Noero combines this subject with a different war, the one against AIDS/HIV, with its still devastating effect on the South African population, and in particular the many women from New Brighton who died. The core idea in the development of Red Location's project was culture and its productions. Thanks to this choice, many ways of thinking and doing architecture in the city have developed. *"By following this path we have the potential to create spaces which are common and enjoyed by all. The potential economic benefits will be significant as local people can take charge of their own lives and express themselves through a form of cultural exchange over which they have control precisely because it is about their own lives and their lived experiences"* (Noero, 2012).

Hamburg, Eastern Cape; on the second, of the same dimensions, a huge map in scale 1:100 of *Red Location Cultural Precinct*'s project[5]. The tapestry's title is *Keiskamma After Guernic*. It recalls through explicit quotes, and has the same dimensions, of Picasso's masterpiece. The subject is again one of death and suffering, but in this case it refers to the devastating effect that HIV has on the South African population and to the many women died of AIDS in New Brighton. The second panel shows a hand-drawn map by Noero of the stratification of existing, built and planned components of the project. It questions the spatial relations between the elements and traces the movement over time of inhabitants and tourists on a random day. The map is voluntarily over-written and retraces on diagrams elements such as the city traffic, playground actions and business areas. The drawing is a representation of the connections and complexities between the parts; shack dwellers, homes, social houses, museums, libraries, archives, art galleries, theatres, areas for shows, meetings and conferences, football fields and the arts and crafts school.

The panels have a twofold relation: they tell us about their complexities, the tapestry through an artistic expression, while the map with a spatial transposition. The former shows us what the map questions in its expression. Both make available their surface for a common ground of coexistence, made of art, architecture and the social nature of spatial production, as a space of '*contradiction and totality*'.
In this work, Noero clarifies the architect's active role in terms of social. His conduct is strongly guided by a sense of responsibility towards the inhabitants and by integrity in respect to the insane, disruptive legacy of apartheid. Noero's work expresses a way to mediate among extreme conditions and offers a space for democracy.
"*A map was not intended to represent the shape of the Earth but to list the cities and the peoples that you come across*" (Eco, 2013).

"Different Worlds; Transformation of Red Location and Keiskamma After Guernica" Venice, Biennale, 2012

Common ground

The term *Common Ground* defines *"the shared space in which two or more people declare to have probably found a meeting point"*[1], as stated by David Chipperfield at the 13th *Mostra Internazionale di Architettura della Biennale di Venezia*. In Red Location that place is spatial representation of an idea, because everything comes from earth and in it we can find the founding act, the *"sulcus primogenius"*, which establishes the city and distinguishes the known from the unknown by identifying the place. Because beyond the furrow there is no spatial organization; and where there is no organization there is no knowledge and there can be no action (Benevolo, 1994).
We also add that where there is no possibility of action or knowledge, there is no freedom.
With his work, Noero sets the spatial coordinates in which the community shall build its own plans of action, starting from an ancient principle, from a cultural project that evokes several visions of the world, in the sense of possibility.[2]
"It is difficult to imagine a situation when the formal order of the universe could be reduced to a diagram of two intersecting co-ordinates in one plane. Yet this is exactly what did happen in antiquity: the Roman who walked along the 'cardo' knew that his walk was the axis round which the sun turned, and that if he followed the 'decumanus', he was following the sun's course. The whole universe and its meaning could be spelt out of his civic institutions - so he was at home in it."[3]
As those axes were able to bend to the environmental and contextual needs, finding in the same space the features of a model inclined to be anchored to the territory, in the same way Noero rediscovers those bends

1. *Le molte vie di David Chipperfield*, L. Bossi, DomusWeb, 07/05/2012.
2. In relation to the sense of possibility, we refer to the words of Musli in *The Man Without Qualities*: "[…] if there is a sense of reality, and no one will doubt that it has its justification for existing, then there must also be something we can call a sense of possibility. Whoever has it does not say, for instance: Here this or that has happened, will happen, must happen; but he invents: Here this or that might, could or ought to happen. If he is told that something is the way it is, he will think: Well, it could probably just as well be otherwise. So the sense of possibility could be defined outright as the ability to conceive of everything there might be just as well, and to attach no more importance to what is than to what is not".
3. *The idea of a Town: the Anthropology of Urban Form in Rome, Italy and the Ancient World*, J. Rykwert, Faber&Faber, 1976, p.168.

Fabrizio Pusceddu

in a complex system of relations, in which the complexity is not just given, but is a consequence of an intimate and at the same time collective effort, putting together space, memory and action.

Relations between people and places are a consequence of the meanings we give to things; this essentially planning operation is the result of providing an active role to the subjects in the space, as the driving force of new and spontaneous processes.

In this scope, the *common ground* becomes public space, in the dynamic tension between personal and collective, where the urban plan identifies the limits of space as possibility. "*The common ground* – Chipperfield stated during the opening speech of the Biennale he directed – *implies a shared territory in a context of differences. This topic identifies the search for common elements within something apparently diverse, and it helps us to elaborate the strategies to face our common condition and our unusually constant need to feel ourselves part of a world which is bigger than the one necessary to individual well-being.*"

In this project presented at the Biennale di Venezia 2012, Noero reads history acknowledging what Calvino identifies, making of it a rhetoric figure, as the *plague*.

"*(...) But maybe this lack of substance is not to be found in images or in language alone, but in the world itself. This plague strikes also at the lives of people and the history of nations. It makes all histories formless, random, confused, with neither beginning nor end. My discomfort arises from the loss of form that I can think of - an idea of literature.*"[4]

Red Location's endeavour is not an inconsistent representation; it is a determined but open drawing. In this drawing we bear the responsibility of fixing a starting point, a "bibliography", where the drawing's layout becomes *common ground* itself, and transforms the land in signs, soaked both by architectural history and the history of men.

It is the proof of an idea in which "*shapes and structures are not only limitation and constraint, but represent also freedom at the service of men's imagination and need to act: the need to represent space and reality cannot be put in contrast with human's creativity; it has to be conceived again as one of the ways and modalities in which it is expressed. It is wrong to consider that the rights of what we call reality can be respected only referring to a model representing it as a combination of objects defined in every part, that men are limited to represent*

and stare at: it is much more appropriate and functional to conceive it as a plot of information, a starting point giving birth to a series of multiple interpretations and manipulations, open to almost unlimited possibilities of transformation."[5]
We rediscover this plot in the work of the Keiskamma Women's Project who manufactured the tapestry exposed at the Biennale. Here, the *common ground* is expressed through art, highlighting that claiming a space is not an exclusive physical condition but rather the need of being part of a community in which it is possible to share ideas not necessarily endorsed by everybody. The *common ground* is therefore an expression, made of ideas, the power of being able to express an opinion not only built on thoughts but also on actions. We are not dealing with a forced fusion, but with an act of reconciliation of different, silent stories which, through The Tapestry, can live and be understood in other very different cultural contexts as well. Under this perspective, the connections between Noero's great project and The Keiskamma Trust's work are deep-rooted. Both agree on representing freedom as *the right to be and remain different within the same common ground* (Bauman) rather than the uniformity of life-styles, or the right to equality. In this scope, Red Location represents a *negotiorum gestio*, a declaration of responsible awareness in regards to reality. This responsibility is enclosed in the recovery of hope in planning, where "*the project is the strongest connection between men, reality and history.*"[6]
In this way, the project can become expression of dissent or, to put it in another way, of openness to disagreement, and renouncing to it would mean giving up hope. Therefore, the *common ground* provides the conditions for the project and becomes project itself: in order that the meeting ground is not an exclusive assignment of the physical boundary delimitation but rather the interpretation of a social space that achieves its full shape with the aid of urban features. A context in which roads, in their wise

---

4. *Six Memories for the Next Millennium*, I. Calvino, Harvard University press, Cambridge, Massachusetts, 1988, p. 57.
5. *L'epistemologia del progetto come cultura della complessità*, S. Tagliagambe, in *La cultura politecnica*, M. Bertoldini, Bruno Mondadori, Milano, 2007, pp. 117-151.
6. *La speranza progettuale: ambiente e società*, T. Maldonado, Einaudi, Torino, 1970
"*When dissent gives up hope, or lacks planning, it is not dangerous for the forces of consent; on the contrary, it can also become of of its subtler expressions*" (p.66).
On the other side, the goal of professional revolutionaries is usually to gain power, not to make revolutions: their speeches are meaningful, gestural, rather than operational or defining a plan; rebels of all times (anabaptists, millenarians, mystics, anarchists ,etc.) love insurrections more than the world they could lead to (p.111). They add an aesthetic component to politics: "for the pleasure, undoubtedly detoxifying, of living a 'tragischer Monat' (Munster, 1532), a 'semana trágica' (Barcelona, 1909), or a 'semaine de Mai'(Paris, 1968), they are willing to jeopardize the feasibility of a surely less troubled, but probably much more effective action" (p.112).

organization, dilatation and anchoring to the ground, define a non-contemplative landscape.

A system in which different organizations within the same context not necessarily exclude themselves but can coexist and prove to be compatible, following the phenomenon defined by Varela and Maturana[7] as the 'operational closure' towards the human beings' ability to preserve and replicate their internal structure, their identity.

As in biology, these processes are dynamic and deeply linked to the definition of relations through action.

"There is no structured information on the outside, it becomes information only by forming itself through my body, by transforming my body, which is called action."[8]

The project therefore stimulates action and by doing this it activates relations of unaware shapes and modalities in a process of acknowledgment.

Finally, if we talk about a *system*, Red Location is not an amalgam of juxtaposed elements connected by laws of linear randomness but an organism characterized by principles of hierarchic and retroactive nature. This network of relations concerns all the system's constitutive elements and allows the identity's and organization's preservation, in a context of ceaseless (endogenous and exogenous) modifications to which the object is exposed.[9]

This process occurs not without the predictable, sometimes tough, resistances within a reality strongly marked by its history, which finds the evolutionary process in the definition of a complexity represented by the strength of the relations between its parts rather than by the sum of the single elements. This complexity is perfectly represented in the planimetry hand-drawn by Jo Noero, able more than any other image to describe the ´project"'s creative force in the space.

---

7. *The Tree of Knowledge. The Biological Roots of Human Understanding*, H. Maturana and F. Varela, Shambhala, Boston, 1984. *"First, the molecular components of a cellular autopoietic unity must be dynamically related in a network of ongoing interactions. [...] Now what is distinctive about this cellular dynamics compared with any other collection of molecular transformations in natural processes? Interestingly, this cell metabolism produces components which make up the network of transformations that produced them. Some of these components form a boundary, a limit to this network of transformations* (p. 44).
"*Organization denotes those relations that must exist between the components of a system for it to be a member of a specific class. Structure denotes the components and relations that actually constitute a particular unity and make its organization real.*" (p. 47)
8. Ibid. Chapter VII
9. Referring to *The General Systems Theory*, as explained by L.U.Ulivi in *Strutture del mondo: il pensiero sistemico come specchio di una realtà complessa*. Il Mulino, Bologna, 2010.

"Keiskamma After Guernica"; Venice Biennale 2012: Common ground/Different worlds; the Keiskamma Women's Project; 7.8×3.5m Tapestry, mixed media, various hand stitched textiles

Bibliography

Ballantyne A., *Architecture Theory, A Reader in Philosophy and Culture*, Bloomsbury Academic, 2005
Bossi L., *Le molte vie di David Chipperfield*, DomusWeb, May, 2012
Calvino I., *Invisible cities*, A Helen and Kurt Wolff Book, London, 1976, p.96
Calvino I., *Six Memories for the Next Millennium*, Harvard University press, Cambridge, Massachusetts, 1988, p. 57
Carroll L., *The Complete Illustrated Works*, Gramercy Books, NewYork, 1982, p. 727
Choay F., "Le règne de l'urbain et la mort de la ville", in *La Ville. Art et architecture en Europe. 1870-1993*, Éditions du Centre Pompidou, Paris, 1994
Desmond T., *No Future Without Forgiveness*, Doubleday, New York, 1999
Eco U., *Storia delle terre e dei luoghi leggendari*, Bompiani, Milan, 2013
Eicker, K., "Red Location Cultural Precinct, Noero Wolff Architects", in *Architectural record*, 2012
Findley L., "Building Memory: The Museum of Struggle", in B*uilding Change: Architecture, Politics and Cultural Agency*, Routledge, London, 2005, pp. 122-160
Findley L., Ogbu L. (co-author), "Becoming Visible: Appropriating the Spaces of Apartheid South Africa", in *Consuming Architecture*, Routledge, London, 2014
Geddes P., *Cities in Evolution: an introduction to the town planning movement and to the study of civics*, Williams & Norgate, London, 1915
Giedion S., *Architektur und Gemeinschaft*, 1956. Italian translation: *Breviario di architettura*, Bollati Boringhieri, Turin, 2008
Heath K. Wm., *Vernacular Architecture and Regional Design: Cultural Process and Environmental Response*, Mass. Architectural Press, Burlington, 2009
Huyssen A., *Twilight Memories: Marking Time in a Culture of Amnesia*, Routledge, London, 1995
Huyssen A., "Present Pasts: Media, Politics, Amnesia", in *Public Culture*, Duke University Press, Durham, NC, 2000, p. 38
Jacobs J., *Vita e morte delle grandi città*, Piccola Biblioteca Einaudi Ns, Bologna, 2009
LeDoux J., *Ansia*, Raffaello Cortina Editore, Milan, 2016
Lefebvre H., *The Production of Space*, Blackwell, Oxford, 1991
Lepik A., *Small Scale, Big Change: New Architectures of Social*, New York Museum of Modern Art, 2010
Low I., "Space and Transformation", in *Digest of South African Architecture*, Cape Town, 2003
Maciocco G. Tagliagambe S., *La città possibile, Territorialità e comunicazione nel progetto urbano*, Dedalo, Bari, 1997
Maldonado T., *La speranza progettuale, ambiente e società*, Einaudi, Torino, 1970
Mandela N., *Long Walk to Freedom*, Little, Brown and Company, Boston, 1994
Marini S., Corbellini G., *Recycled Theory: Dizionario illustrato/Illustrated Dictionary*, Quodlibet, Macerata, 2016, p. 35
Marotta A., *Archeologie. Il progetto e la memoria del tempo*, Edil stampa, Roma, 2015, p. 65
Maturana H., Varela F., *The Tree of Knowledge. The Biological Roots of Human Understanding*, Shambhala, Boston, 1984

Mehrotra R., "Re-thinking the informal city", in *AREA*, 2013, n.128, pp. 6-11

Melvin J., "Living Space; Red Location's Evolving cultural precinct explores ideas about placemaking and the African urban realm", in *Architectural Review*, 2011, pp. 44-53

Montanini M., *Redenzione forzata; Sviluppo, post-apartheid e pratiche di appropriazione a Red Location*, PhD in Social and Political Change, XXIX Ciclo, 2016

Moronell C., *Architecture and Transformation: Post-colonial conditions, post-modernist approaches. Situating the architectural project of hybridity within the post-colonial African city*, October 2011 https://pdfs.semanticscholar.org/eb06/7b3455e3681ea7da0bc31c70111af0865b54.pdf

Morojele, M., "Space and Identity; From the Grassroots to the Global", in *Digest of South African Architecture*, Cape Town, 2003

Murray N., "Reframing the contemporary, architecture and the postcolony", in *Contemporary South African Architecture in a Landscape of Transition* (by Deckler T., Graupner A., Rasmus H.), Double Storey Books, Lansdowne, 2006

Noero J., "Winners: Noero Wolff Architects, Architect's statement", in *South African Architect*, June 1999

Noero J., "Red Location Innovation" in *South African Architect*, Nov/Dec 1999

Noero J., "Architecture and Memory", in *Global Cities: Cinema, Architecture, and Urbanism in a Digital Age*, ed. by Linda Krause and Patrice Petro, Rutgers University Press, Piscataway, New Jersey, 2003

Noero J., Sorrel J., *Jo Noero: The Everyday and the Extraordinary: three decades of architecture*, ADA Pub, 2009

Noero Wolff Architects, "PELIP houses", in *Divisare*, 2011

Noero J., "Red Location Precinct Phase 2", in *Digest of South African Architecture*, n. 17, 2012

Noero J., "Housing in the post modern world", in Faiferri M., Bartocci S. (2012), *Housing the Emergency - The Emergency of Housing*, ListLab, Trento, 2012, p. 148

Perryer S., *10 Years 100 Artists: Art in a Democratic South Africa*, Struik, Cape Town, 2004

Rykwert J., *The idea of a Town: the Anthropology of Urban Form in Rome, Italy and the Ancient World*, Faber&Faber, 1976, p.168

Secchi B., *La città dei ricchi e la città dei poveri*, Laterza, Roma, 2013

Smith, M., "Interment: Re-framing", in *Kronos*, 2016, p. 42

Smithson A., Smithson P., *Ordinariness and Light*, MIT Press, Cambridge, Massachusetts, 1970

Steenkamp A., "Apartheid to Democracy: Representation and Politics in the Voortrekker Monument and Red Location Museum", in *Arq: Architectural Research*, Quarterly, 2006, pp. 249-254

Tagliagambe S., "L'epistemologia del progetto come cultura della complessità", *La cultura politecnica 2 (by Bertoldini M.)*, Bruno Mondadori, Milano, 2007, pp. 117-151

Ulivi L.U., *Strutture del mondo: il pensiero sistemico come specchio di una realtà complessa*, Il Mulino, Bologna, 2010

Vladislavic I., Goldblatt D., *Doppia negazione*, Contrasto, Milano, 2012

Walsh F., *South Africa, A Narrative History*, Kodansha, New York, 1999

Interviews with author, Noeroarchitects, Cape town (2013)
Interviews with author, Noeroarchitects, Venice's Biennale Inaugural statement: "Everyday and the Extraordinary", (2014)
Recent works by Jo Noero Architects, Master in Sustainable And Affordable Housing, DADU, UNISS, Complesso di Santa Chiara, Alghero
Interviews with author, Noeroarchitects, Scientific School, ILS Innovative Learning Spaces, DADU, UNISS, Porto Conte Ricerche, Località Tramariglio, Alghero, 2017

www.ecourbanlab.it
https://www.ilpost.it/lucamolinari/2013/12/27/tornare-allafrica-alla-architettura/
https://placesjournal.org/article/south-africa-from-township-to-town/
https://placesjournal.org/article/red-and-gold-a-tale-of-two-apartheid-museums/
https://www.architecturalrecord.com/articles/7900-red-location-cultural-precinct?v=preview
http://media1.mweb.co.za/iziko/iziko/press/20090820.htm

editorial series:
Sustainable and affordable housing

editor in chief:
Massimo Faiferri

scientific-editorial committee:
Enric Batlle
Gonçalo Byrne
Anne Lacaton
Joe Noero
Federico Soriano
Jean Philippe Vassal

http://housing.aaamaster.it/

for info please contact:
DADU, Dipartimento di Architettura, Design e Urbanistica,
Palazzo del Pou Salit - Piazza Duomo 6, 07041 Alghero (SS).
e-mail aaamaster@uniss.it
www.architettura.uniss.it/ita/Didattica/Master

Collegio dei docenti Master "Sustainable and affordable housing"

Direttore del Master
Massimo Faiferri - Università di Sassari

Collegio del Master
Valter Caldana, Universidade Presiteriana Mackenzie Sao Paulo
Arnaldo Cecchini- Università di Sassari
Enrico Cicalò - Università di Sassari
Josep Mias Gifrè - Università di Sassari
Alessandro Plaisant - Università di Sassari
Ignasi Perez Arnal - Visiting professor presso l'Università di Sassari
Pedro Rodrigues, Universidade Tecnica de Lisboa
Silvia Serreli - Università di Sassari
Stefan Tischer- Università di Sassari

Docenti Tutor
Samanta Bartocci
Mauro Cossu
Filippo De Dominicis
Jacopo Galli
Fabrizio Pusceddu

Sustainable and affordable housing is an international book series founded with the aim of conveying the studies, research and cultural initiatives developed within the international Master's Degree Level 2 of the same name set up at the Department of Architecture, Design and Urbanism of the University of Sassari, in cooperation with the Facultade de Arquitectura of the Universidade Tecnica de Lisboa, the Universidade Presbiteriana of Sao Paulo and the Autonomous Region of Sardinia - Department of Labour, Vocational Training, Cooperation and Social Security.

The series uses a text evaluation system based on an anonymous peer-review by lecturers of the Publisher's Research Committee.

The creation of this series has been possible thanks to the contribution of:

Red Location Cultural Percinct
noeroarchitects

Author
Samanta Bartocci

Editorial Director
Alessandro Franceschini

Published by
LISt Lab
info@listlab.eu
listlab.eu

Art Director& Production
Blacklist Creative, BCN
blacklist-creative.com

Translation
Jacopo Marcomeni

ISBN 9788898774982

**Printed and bound
in the European Union,**
April 2018

All rights reserved
© of LISt Lab edition;
© of the author's texts;
© of the author's images:
Noero Architects archives;

serie **sustainable and affordable
housing collection**

Prohibited total or partial reproduction
of this book by any means, without permission
of the author and Publisher.

Promotion and distribution in Italy
Messaggerie Libri, Spa, Milano,
assistenza.ordini@meli.it;
amministrazione.vendite@meli.it

**International promotion and
distribution**
ACC Book Distribution Ltd
Woodbridge, Suffolk, IP12 4SD, UK
sales@antique-acc.com

**The Scientific Committee of the
issues List**
Eve Blau (Harvard GSD), Maurizio Carta (University of Palermo), Eva Castro (Architectural Association London) Alberto Clementi (University of Chieti), Alberto Cecchetto (University of Venezia), Stefano De Martino (University of Innsbruck), Corrado Diamantini (University of Trento), Antonio De Rossi (University of Torino), Franco Farinelli (University of Bologna), Carlo Gasparrini (University of Napoli), Manuel Gausa (University of Genova), Giovanni Maciocco (University of Sassari/Alghero), Antonio Paris (University of Roma), Mosè Ricci (University of Trento), Roger Riewe (University of Graz), Pino Scaglione (University of Trento), Claudia Battaino (University of Trento), Luca Zecchin (University of Trento).

LISt Lab is an editorial workshop, based in Europe, that works on contemporary issues. LISt Lab not only publishes, but also researches, proposes, promotes, produces, creates networks.

LISt Lab is a green company committed to respect the environment. Paper, ink, glues and all processings come from short supply chains and aim at limiting pollution. The print run of books and magazines is based on consumption patterns, thus preventing waste of paper and surpluses. LISt Lab aims at the responsibility of the authors and markets, towards the knowledge of a new publishing culture based on resource management.